D1035327

AMERICAN CRIME FICTION

American Crime Fiction

Studies in the Genre

Edited by

Brian Docherty

St. Martins Press   New York

First published in the United States of America in 1988

Printed and bound in Great Britain

ISBN 0–312–01685–9

Library of Congress Cataloging-in-Publication Data
American crime fiction: studies in the genre/edited by Brian Docherty.
p. cm.
Bibliography: p.
Includes index.
ISBN 0–312–01685–9: $40.00
1. Detective and mystery stories, American—History and criticism.
2. Crime and criminals in literature. I. Docherty, Brian.
PS374.D4A44 1988
813′.0872′09–dc19

87–30759
CIP

Burgess
PS
374
.D4
A44
1988

c.1

Contents

Contents

Preface

This volume offers critical and theoretical perspectives on one of the most popular and enduring literary genres: American crime fiction. There are essays on Edgar Allan Poe, Dashiell Hammett, Raymond Chandler, James M. Cain, Mickey Spillane, George V. Higgins and Jerome Charyn, covering the period from 1840 to 1980. Hammett and Chandler have two essays each, reflecting their importance and lasting influence on the genre.

Each essay deals with a major aspect or concept associated with crime fiction. A variety of reading strategies are employed to interrogate these texts, illustrating both the range of approaches available, and the fact that modern literary theory can usefully be applied to any text or genre. Students of crime fiction seeking new readings, and readers interested in modern approaches to literature, such as psychoanalytic theories, Marxist theory, semiotics and linguistic theory, will find this book useful and informative. The essays are all new, and have been specially written for this volume by leading academics.

Acknowledgements

Thanks are due to Graham Greenglass for his artistic guidance, to Lesley Bloom for contributions to typing, to Frances and Leon Kacher for their invaluable assistance, and to Hannah Green, Graham Eyre, Valery Rose, Clive Bloom and Frances Arnold.

Notes on the Contributors

Christopher Bentley has published extensively on English and American literature from the seventeenth to the twentieth centuries, and on the history of medicine. He has taught in British, Canadian and Australian universities and now lectures at the University of Sydney.

Richard Bradbury teaches in the Department of English at the University of Warwick.

Gary Day did his doctorate on the early works of Charles Dickens. He teaches English and Drama in Brighton, and is a contributor to *The Dickensian*.

Brian Docherty is a founder member of Lumiere Press. Having graduated from Middlesex Polytechnic, he now teaches in London and is completing research into American poetry.

Michael J. Hayes teaches at the Lancashire Polytechnic. Besides American crime fiction, his research interests include Disraeli's early writings.

Peter Humm teaches at Thames Polytechnic. He is one of the editors of *Literature and History*, and of the recent collection *Popular Fictions: Essays in Literature and History*.

Stephen Knight is Associate Professor in English at the University of Sydney and has published essays and books on medieval and modern literature. His books include *Form and Ideology* and *Arthurian Literature and Society*.

Odette L'Henry Evans is Principal Lecturer in Comparative Literature and French at the Polytechnic of North London.

Christopher Rollason is a graduate of Trinity College, Cambridge, and the University of York. He is a lecturer in the Department of Anglo-American Studies, Coimbra University, Portugal. His publications include articles on Poe and Balzac; Wordsworth, Byron and Shelley; and Bob Dylan.

Mike Woolf teaches literature at Tottenham College of Technology, London, and writes on cultural matters for BBC Radio 4.

1

Introduction: Hard Talk and Mean Streets

BRIAN DOCHERTY

This collection of essays on American crime fiction is not an encyclopedia or compendium on the subject. It seeks instead to offer some critical and theoretical perspectives on a genre which has enjoyed popular support and huge sales figures for over sixty years, but which has never attained academic respectability. Dashiell Hammett is not regarded as 'literature' and thus is not generally taught in the university–polytechnic system, although he probably had a decisive influence on Ernest Hemingway, who *is* taught, and is recognised as a major figure in modern literature, credited with innovations in respect of style, technique and subject matter. Nine essays cannot possibly deal with an entire genre and its origins, developments, offshoots, blind alleys and variations. Nevertheless, we offer a selection of essays each of which deals with a major aspect or concept encountered in or generated by the genre.

The book therefore opens with Christopher Rollason's essay (Ch. 2) on Edgar Allan Poe's Auguste Dupin, perhaps not the very first detective in fiction, but undoubtedly the model for a great many later sleuths, investigators and private eyes. The essay is neither literary history nor evaluation, but a theoretical interrogation of Poe's procedures and strategies.

Peter Humm's essay (Ch. 3) moves into the twentieth century and the more familiar territory of the classic 'hard-boiled' thrillers of Hammett and Chandler. It seeks to present this new type of writing not as a sport or an aberration but as a form of writing with much in common with other writing of the period and informed by similar concerns. Peter Humm shows that a variety of authors had a similar perspective on writing and the nature of the relationship between literature and society in the Depression years, and that the common concern was to record, as objectively as possible, social life as the authors saw it.

Gary Day (Ch. 4) focuses on Hammett's unnamed yet representative figure, the Continental Op. He examines the nature of Hammett's representation of reality by focusing on the use Hammett makes of an apparently plain language and a 'realistic' mode of writing. Psychoanalytic techniques are employed to demonstrate that this 'realistic' language is in fact highly mediated and has no privileged access to 'truth'. In fact the Op never proves anything, and the reader is obliged to accept his word: his *parole*.

Christopher Bentley's essay on Hammett (Ch. 5) focuses on *Red Harvest*, his first and politically most radical book. This essay offers a political analysis of the Continental Op's activities in 'Poisonville', using this to provide an analysis of Hammett's political views. Hammett has the reputation of being a left-wing radical in a very conservative genre, and the essay asks to what extent this view is justified.

Stephen Knight's essay on Raymond Chandler (Ch. 6) focuses on Chandler's hero Philip Marlowe, and the combination of values and attitudes which serve to define Marlowe. Marlowe is very different from the Continental Op or Sam Spade, just as Hammett's San Francisco is different from Chandler's Los Angeles. Marlowe has a code of values, even ideals, which seem oddly un-American in the hard-boiled America of violent crime and sudden death.

Richard Bradbury's essay on James M. Cain (Ch. 7) stays in California, but a much 'hotter' California of throbbing sexual passion, which turns to violence all too easily. It is a long way from the pure reason of Dupin to the murderous passion of *The Postman Always Rings Twice*. Perhaps Cain is offering an explanation of why the Continental Op and Marlowe are virtually asexual figures, afraid of involvement with women. Cain also offers a reversal of perspective in another important area, that of narrative viewpoint. His books are in a sense twice-told tales, being transcriptions of confessions by a convicted criminal.

Odette L'Henry Evans (Ch. 8) writes on Mickey Spillane's Mike Hammer, a private eye in New York. Spillane and his Cold War 'heroes' such as Mike Hammer are given a reading which by disregarding more traditional reading strategies, and the relation of crime fiction to some hypothetical 'great tradition', actually promotes the status of Spillane's writing. A semiotic approach which concentrates on the structure of the text is used to understand the system of codes which produce theme and meaning. The text is revealed in its plurality, the same and yet always new.

Michael Hayes, in his essay on George V. Higgins (Ch. 9), offers a linguistic analysis of the books which demonstrates that the struggle between different criminals or between police and thieves is really a struggle for control of discourse. He offers an explanation for the paradox that crime novels, supposedly about action, incident, and movement, are predominantly made up of speech or reported speech. He also shows that Higgins's discourse has a logic which is artistically satisfying because it allows the reader a sense of healing through the consumption and exploration of abrasive human relationships.

Mike Woolf (Ch. 10) writes on Jerome Charyn, a contemporary Jewish writer, also New York based. A reading of the majority of crime books would never give the impression that America has a rich and vibrant Jewish culture. Indeed, the ethnic diversity of American life is strangely absent from the 'classic' writings of Hammett and Chandler *et al*. Rather than this mythic, depopulated America, Charyn affirms the tribal nature of American life, especially in the great cities such as New York. Each tribe or religious/ethnic grouping has its own territory and its own code of laws which are enforced within its boundaries. Conflict arises both internally when the laws are transgressed and externally when different codes come into conflict. The tribe also functions as a metaphor for the operations of American society as a whole, and criminality becomes a mirror image of 'official' capitalism. The essay also illuminates another aspect of Charyn's writing, its myth-making and spiritualising tendencies. In this sense, of course, Charyn belongs to a long tradition of Jewish writing. He uses the detective novel to explore the profane and the profound in a world where the bizarre is normal. Isaac, his hero of many names ('the Shit', the 'Pure', the 'Rabbi', 'the Brave'), is both a holy fool and the dark angel holding back the chaos of an exploding world.

Auguste Dupin by the exercise of pure reason restored order to a bourgeois society temporarily disrupted by crime. In the complex alienated tribal society of the modern world, any moral order reinstated by the detective can only be a temporary illusion. The genre, like the world from which it originated, has been exploded.

2

The Detective Myth in Edgar Allan Poe's Dupin Trilogy

CHRISTOPHER ROLLASON

This essay offers an analysis of Poe's trilogy of tales centred on the detective C. Auguste Dupin: 'The Murders in the Rue Morgue' (1841), 'The Mystery of Marie Rogêt' (1842–3) and 'The Purloined Letter' (1844),[1] with the main emphasis on the first and last.

The present discussion does not aim to place the tales in the history of detective fiction. For Conan Doyle, 'Poe ... was the father of the detective tale';[2] similar opinions are expressed by Paul Valéry (1928),[3] Walter Benjamin (1938),[4] T. S. Eliot (1949),[5] and Jorge Luis Borges (1980), who goes so far as to claim that 'Poe exhausted the genre'.[6] Historians of the genre – Howard Haycraft (1941),[7] Julian Symons (1973)[8] and Jerry Palmer (1978)[9] – have come to much the same conclusion. Examination of precursor and successor eighteenth- and nineteenth-century texts, from Voltaire's *Zadig* (1748) through to Conan Doyle, tends to confirm this view, though space does not permit such an analysis here.[10] Taking the historical perspective as given, the present study aims to consider certain psychological and sociological aspects of the detective figure, as mythical embodiment of a certain conception of the 'full', integrated, conflict-free subject – of what Terry Eagleton (1985) has called 'the bourgeois humanist conception of the subject as free, active, autonomous and self-identical'.[11]

Idealist critics have frequently read Dupin as symbolising the apotheosis of the 'autonomous', 'disinterested' intellect. Thus for Richard Wilbur (1967) 'The Murders in the Rue Morgue' is an allegory of 'a soul's fathoming and ordering of itself', which issues in 'the reintegrated and harmonious consciousness of Dupin'.[12] This type of reading is based on certain ideological notions of the possibility and desirability of a conflict-free subjectivity. It can, however, scarcely fail to appear naïve today, given the Lacan–Derrida polemic over 'The Purloined Letter',[13] which starts out from a psychoanalytic tradition of reading texts in terms of conflict and contradiction.

This tradition begins with Marie Bonaparte's study of Poe (1933). In her reading of 'The Murders in the Rue Morgue', the text signifies not any illusory coherence of the subject, but the persistence of unconscious psychic conflicts. The ape represents the Oedipal father, the locked room the mother's body; the murders correspond to the infant's 'sadistic theory of coitus'.[14] In 'The Purloined Letter' the letter is read as symbolising the child's fantasies about active maternal sexuality.[15] Jacques Lacan's 'Séminaire sur "La Lettre volée"' (1957) goes further than Bonaparte's text in its deconstitution of the illusory monadic subject. The letter is, again,[16] read as a signifier of female desire ('like an immense female body');[17] but, further, the whole tale is read as exemplifying the determining instance of the letter (the signifier) in the unconscious: 'the high degree of determination which the subject receives as it is traversed by a signifier'.[18] The various fictional subjects have their actions assigned to them by the letter, which inserts them into their respective places in the signifying chain of events. Consciousness is thus seen as intersubjective and non-autonomous.

Jacques Derrida's critique of the 'Séminaire' ('Le facteur de la vérité', 1975), while offering itself as a deconstructionist alternative to Lacan's 'metaphysical' discourse, may also be read as taking the process of deconstitution even further. For Derrida the key structure in 'The Purloined Letter' is the double; as in Freud's 'The "Uncanny"' (1919),[19] the motif is seen as productive of fear and disturbance. 'The Purloined Letter' is read as a 'labyrinth of doubles',[20] in which subjects double subjects and letters letters, and definitive signification is endlessly deferred; any notion of the unitary subject is thus seen as invalidated by a text which itself has no unitary 'meaning'.

In a different direction, recent sociological readings have exposed the divine detective as an ideological construct corresponding to determinate class interests. Stephen Knight (1980) sees Dupin as the first literary instance of the detective as 'intelligent, infallible, isolated hero';[21] the texts are seen as palliating the anxieties of the bourgeois intellectual reader, objectively peripheral within his own class, making him feel that his own social group is uniquely equipped to interpret the world. Jerry Palmer, in his genre study *Thrillers* (1978), sees the Dupin tales as the first fully developed instance of the thriller genre (of which the nineteenth-century detective story is a sub-genre). The basic structure of the genre is: competitive individualism versus conspiracy.[22] The competitive, individualistic, isolated 'hero' represents 'the social order that already exists';[23] society as it stands is seen as 'a good place'[24] and as 'in the normal run of things, devoid of conflict'.[25] Order is disrupted in the thriller plot by a pathological, alien conspiracy, typically fronted by a specially evil 'villain'.[26] The source of disturbance is located either outside society (in foreigners) or in degenerate individuals – that is, 'forces which exist within society, but which have no social origin'.[27] The hero intervenes to crush the conspiracy and 'restore normality';[28] he thus functions as a social saviour.[29] The thriller–detective genre emerges as inherently conservative, tending to perpetuate the existing order by naturalising it. Palmer offers sociological explanations for the genre's popularity; competitive individualism is seen as fomented by the market economy,[30] while the fear of conspiracy is linked to the threat of working-class insurrection.[31] For both Knight and Palmer, then, the detective story offers the middle-class reader an imaginary palliation for real social anxieties.

With the above social context in mind, the textual construction of Dupin as subject will now be considered in detail. In all three tales, the material is organised so as to give maximum prominence to Dupin's intellectual qualities – to what the narrator in 'The Murders in the Rue Morgue' calls 'some very remarkable features in the mental character of my friend' (p. 724). In this tale Dupin is differentiated from both the narrator and the Prefect of Police as the *only* person competent to solve the mystery. The narrator is presented as an 'average' middle-class intellectual (and stand-in for the intended probable reader); he is inferior to Dupin, though privileged in relation to the police (since he, and not the Prefect, is the recipient of Dupin's explanation). What Palmer calls the thriller triad of 'Amateur', 'Professional' and 'Bureaucrat'[32] is thus constituted. The Prefect is a Bureaucrat, unable to handle anything outside the limits of his training and experience; the narrator is an Amateur, of only ordinary competence; Dupin is a Professional, in the sense not of making detection his profession, but of applying analytic rigour and specialist knowledge. 'The Murders in the Rue Morgue' repeats much the same formula; 'The Purloined Letter', however, throws Dupin's intellect into even greater relief by introducing a 'professional' villain – the Minister D—, whom Dupin has by the end 'outwitted' (p. 993) – and by constructing a complex hierarchy of intellectual levels. Lacan has shown how the text presents two triangular situations: the first, in the royal boudoir; the second, in D—'s 'hotel'. In each case, there is 'a look which sees nothing' (the King; the police); 'a look which sees that the first one sees nothing' (the Queen; D—); and 'the third which sees that both those two looks leave what is to be hidden exposed for the one who wants to take it' (D—; Dupin). [33] In the second triangle, D— is reduced from the first degree of vision to the second; Dupin is, conversely, raised to the status of having the only consistently all-seeing vision in the text. The detective thus becomes a model reader, an exemplary decoder and interpreter of the world. [34]

On closer examination, however, Dupin proves to be a less homogeneous, 'integrated' figure than appears at first sight. By the end of 'The Murders in the Rue Morgue', the naïve or first-time reader may have forgotten that the infallible, rigorous analyst (who defeats both ape and Prefect) exhibits certain inconsistencies hardly compatible with the Dupin who was introduced at the beginning – although certain critics, such as Mireille Vincent (1975), have noticed this 'disturbing contradiction'. [35] Dupin initially appears in 'The Murders in the Rue Morgue' as an unstable, incoherent subject. His imagination is 'wild', and he is subject to 'fantastic gloom'; he is prone to 'wild whims', such as an obsession with darkness which the narrator terms a 'freak of fancy' and a '*bizarrerie*' (p. 532). All the above suggests that Dupin is marked by splitting and disintegrative tendencies; the narrator admits that an outsider might have seen them both as 'madmen' (p. 532), and suggests that Dupin's eccentricities may have been 'the result of an excited, or perhaps of a diseased intelligence' (p. 533).

Besides, Dupin is further characterised as *double*: 'I often dwelt meditatively upon the old philosophy of the Bi-Part Soul, and amused myself with the fantasy of a double Dupin – the creative and the resolvent' (p. 533). He has a double voice, alternating between 'tenor' and 'treble' (p. 533); it is the latter, anomalous voice, accompanied by an 'abstract' manner, that is the medium for his moments of analytic explanation, *including* the explanation of the murders ('I have already spoken of his abstract manner at such times' – p. 548). He has thus to split himself, to make himself other and assume his treble voice in order to produce his feats of ratiocination; this hardly suggests that detection, as Wilbur has it, leads to a 'reintegrated' subjectivity. Doubling is, besides – as has often been noted[36] – a theme inscribed across the text of 'The Murders in the Rue Morgue'; Dupin is doubled by the narrator, Dupin and the sailor by the ape, and the Dupin–narrator couple by the L'Espanaye and ape–sailor pairs. The double motif will be further considered below, with special reference to the doubling between Dupin and the ape; it will return with a vengeance in 'The Purloined Letter'. For the moment, however, attention will be concentrated on another instance of doubleness in the texts: Dupin's methodology.

The detective is double in his methods; as Knight points out,[37] he is both artist and scientist – 'creative' and 'resolvent' ('Rue Morgue', p. 533), 'imaginative' and 'analytic' (p. 531). Dupin is expert on both literary and scientific topics, from Rousseau (p. 568) to the nebular cosmogony (p. 536). This multifaceted erudition may appear to constitute him as a 'perfect', 'balanced' subject; whether, however, the texts in practice hold his artist and scientist sides in balance[38] is highly dubious.

Dupin employs two principal methods, which operate *discontinuously* across the series. The first is 'scientific', the method of empirical deduction. In 'The Murders in the Rue Morgue' and 'The Mystery of Marie Rogêt', the mysteries are solved thanks to his deductive ability and possession of specialist information. By his explicit reference to Cuvier ('Rue Morgue', p. 559), Dupin places himself in a certain emergent tradition of science conceived as the description and classification of objects (he shows the narrator Cuvier's 'minute anatomical and generally descriptive account of the large fulvous Ourang-Outang' – p. 559). The English term 'scientist' had just been coined, by Thomas Whewell in 1840;[39] Dupin may be situated in the context of what Raymond Williams (1976) calls a model of science in terms of 'neutral methodical observer and external object of study'.[40] Indeed, the detective hero may be seen as anticipating the 'heroic-positivistic' model of the scientist that was to become dominant in the twentieth century (the scientist as disinterested, isolated, competitive investigator whose activity necessarily contributes to social progress).[41]

The second method, however, is best described as 'imaginative'; it involves placing oneself in the other's position in order to reconstruct his or her thoughts. It is thus that Dupin solves the mystery in 'The Purloined Letter'. This method, with its tendency to leap the subject–object divide, may be seen as a variant of the Romantic concept of the imagination; one may compare Shelley's *A Defence of Poetry* (1821): 'A man, to be greatly good, must imagine intensely and comprehensively; he must put himself in the place of another, and of many others',[42] or Keats's 1818 letter to R. Woodhouse: 'As to the poetical Character ... it is not itself.... A Poet ... has no identity – he is continually in for – and filling some other Body.'[43] In reconstituting the other's thoughts, Dupin becomes that other.

The empirical method dominates the first two tales, but the imaginative method is primary in 'The Purloined Letter'. Indeed, in that tale the empirical method is actually denigrated; the Prefect's 'most powerful microscope' (p. 980) and knowledge of *recherché* hiding places fail to lead to discovery of the letter. There is, in Knight's words, 'a crucial change in the detective's methodology'[44] between 'The Mystery of Marie Rogêt' and 'The Purloined Letter'. Thus, rather than synthesising the 'analytic' and 'imaginative' methods, the series holds them in *im*balance; it is a question not of achieved equilibrium, but of unresolved tension.

The two methods will now be examined in greater detail. The clearest instances of the empirical method occur in 'The Murders in the Rue Morgue', where the ape and sailor are tracked down through the study of their traces. The ourang-outang is identified through examination of a tuft of its hair, found between the fingers of Mme L'Espanaye (p. 558) and the indentations of its fingers on Mlle L'Espanaye's throat (pp. 558–9); the sailor, via a ribbon dropped by the lightning-rod (p. 561), with its tell-tale knot. Dupin establishes that 'no animal but an Ourang-Outang ... could have impressed the indentations' (p. 559); and that the sailor must be from a Maltese vessel, since the knot 'is peculiar to the Maltese' (p. 561). The method may be summarised as follows: an object is found; its characteristics are established; specialist knowledge is applied to place the object within a larger system; the person (or animal) to whom the object belongs is identified. Under this method lie certain epistemological assumptions about situations and objects. For Dupin, to know a situation means to reconstitute its components in such a way that they form a coherent signifying chain ('there was no flaw in any link of the chain' – p. 553). To know an object means, first, to describe it in detail; second, to classify it within a wider paradigm, or series of paradigms. The term 'ourang-outang' is defined by differentiation from its fellow terms in a paradigm that contains 'gorilla', 'baboon', and so on, which is itself inserted in a larger paradigm of the 'mammalia' (p. 559) – including 'man'. Dupin, then, confronts the object on two levels – the syntagmatic and the paradigmatic, to use Saussure's terminology (1916), as modified by Jonathan Culler (1974).[45] The paradigmatic level establishes that the hairs can only belong to an ourang-outang; the syntagmatic level places them in the chain of events that includes the murders. Once the object is thus inserted into these larger structures, Dupin considers the question to be' closed; this, for him, is to know 'the matter as a whole' (p. 545).

None the less, this method is not only empirical, but, in the end, empiricist; Dupin refuses to place the ape in any complex of structures *larger than is absolutely necessary to explain the events*. There is no question of inserting the animal, once classified *à la* Cuvier, into any wider social or historical context. The text answers the question, *how* did the ape get to Paris? (it was captured in Borneo), but not the question, *why*? Dupin never considers the possible existence of an objective historical link binding him to the ape. However, the process which does ultimately link subject to object may be given a name: imperialism. The sailor's presence in 'the Indian Archipelago' (modern Indonesia) (p. 564) is not fortuitous, but dictated by European economic interests: he is French, the 'Maltese vessel' (p. 560) hails from a British colony, and Borneo was colonised by the British and Dutch. The murders are ultimately a consequence of European colonialism; the ape, as a 'valuable animal' (p. 562), is potentially inserted into the commodity structure, yet another object stolen from the colonies for profit (the sailor's 'ultimate design was to sell it' – p. 564).

Dupin's method, in contrast, assumes that objects become knowable once they are inserted into a series of systems which, at a certain point, is cordoned off as a *closed system*. His epistemology is, in this sense, classically empiricist; it is confined by what Lukács, in *History and Class Consciousness* (1923), calls the 'isolated and isolating facts and partial systems' of empiricist discourse.[46] If materialist discourse 'sees the isolated facts of social life as aspects of the historical process and integrates them into a *totality*',[47] and is aware of the 'dialectical relation between subject and object',[48] Dupin's method, in contrast, estranges objects and situations from history and fails to problematise the subject–object relation. By failing to raise crucial questions, his empiricism ultimately walks hand-in-glove with the existing social order.

The imaginative method is introduced in 'The Murders in the Rue Morgue' in the passage on draughts, where it is said that 'the analyst throws himself into the spirit of his opponent, identifies himself therewith' (p. 529). It is exemplified at length in the 'Chantilly episode' (pp. 533–7), where Dupin reconstructs the 'links of the chain' (p. 535) of the narrator's thoughts, giving them back to him as an unbroken signifying chain. It recurs later in the tale when the detective places himself in the sailor's position: 'He will reason thus . . . ' (p. 561); and is also employed in 'The Mystery of Marie Rogêt', as when Dupin reconstructs the naval officer's reactions: 'His natural thought would have been . . . ' (p. 771).

It is in 'The Purloined Letter', however, that this method becomes dominant. In the schoolboy's game of 'even and odd', as described by Dupin, the successful player's method consists of 'an identification of the reasoner's intellect with that of his opponent' (p. 984). The Prefect fails with D— 'by default of this identification' (p. 985), whereas Dupin succeeds, thanks to his belief that he knows the Minister ('I knew him' – p. 988), and that he can therefore put himself in his shoes: 'He must have foreseen, I reflected . . . ' (p. 988). The imaginative method allows the thoughts and actions of the other to appear completely predictable.

By this 'identification' with D—, Dupin effectively subverts his own autonomy as subject; this is one element in the complex process of doubling between detective and criminal, which will be discussed below. Yet, at the same time, the method works in the opposite direction, tending also to confirm the notion of the coherent subject. It rests, after all, on a specific ideology of 'character'. In the game of even and odd, the schoolboy's strategy is based on the definition of his opponent's character: 'how wise, or how stupid, or how good, or how wicked is any one' (p. 984). The key syntactic element here is the copula; the generalising use of 'to be' points to a notion of character as a fixed, metaphysical essence. Similarly, Dupin defines D— in terms of given, innate qualities: 'He is, perhaps, the most really energetic human being now alive' (p. 990); 'D— . . . is a man of nerve' (p. 992); 'he is that *monstrum horrendum*, an unprincipled man of genius' (p. 993). The recurrent copula again indicates the ideology of character, which permits the notion of the predictability of the other. The imaginative method is thus ambivalent in its construction of subjectivity; it *undermines* the illusion of the full subject by crossing the subject–object divide, and yet simultaneously *underwrites* that same illusion through its assumptions about 'character'. However, this kind of ambivalence is not present in the empirical method; the replacement of empiricism by imagination in 'The Purloined Letter' does tend to suggest a certain subversion of the autonomous subject across the cycle.

Analysis will now be focused on Dupin's relation to his various opponents (actual or potential); here too, the notion of the full subject will be seen to undergo textual contestation. It must first be stressed, however, that the texts specify a clear social–economic context for Dupin's combats. The social order which the detective sets out to defend is that of expanding mid-nineteenth-century capitalism, in which elements inherited from feudalism (aristocracy, monarchy) tend to be enlisted in the service of the newly dominant mode of production. Dupin is an aristocrat, a 'Chevalier' ('Marie Rogêt', p. 724), of 'an excellent – indeed of an illustrious family' ('Rue Morgue', p. 531). However, his economic insertion into society undergoes significant changes over the series. When first introduced, he is a down-at-heel aristocratic *rentier*: 'there still remained in his possession a small amount of his patrimony; and, upon the income arising from this, he managed . . . to procure the necessaries of life' (p. 531). But, after meeting the narrator, he accepts his patronage: 'I was permitted to be at the expense of renting and furnishing . . . a . . . mansion' (p. 532). For the moment, Dupin remains on the margins of the market economy; in 'The Murders in the Rue Morgue', no reward is asked for or given – but the ape's commodity status (it fetches 'a very large sum' – p. 568) serves as reminder of the market's existence.

In 'The Mystery of Marie Rogêt', however, Dupin turns businessman; the narrator states rather coyly that the Prefect made the detective 'a direct, and certainly a liberal proposition, the precise nature of which I do not feel myself at liberty to disclose' (p. 728). After the mystery is solved, 'the Prefect fulfilled . . . the terms of his compact with the Chevalier' (p. 772). Dupin, then, does his work and is paid the rate for the job; detection has become a scarce and valuable commodity, which its owner sells dear. The financial element is, finally, specified without embarrassment in 'The Purloined Letter'; Dupin only surrenders the letter on receipt of the Prefect's cheque (p. 983). This incorporation of Dupin into the cash nexus is (as Knight points out[49]) gradual; but, even in 'The

Murders in the Rue Morgue', the social order Dupin is defending is clearly that of contemporary capitalism, with the L'Espanayes with their fat bank account (p. 541) as representatives of the bourgeois order that the ape disturbs. Dupin's gradual transition from patronage to the market corresponds to a wider shift in the social insertion of intellectuals;[50] while nominally an aristocrat, he is in practice absorbed into the capitalist order, anticipating the more fully professionalised Holmes, whose 'ancestors were country squires'.[51] The social order that the detective intervenes to save is essentially the *bourgeois* order.

As potential social saviour, Dupin encounters a series of highly differentiated opponents across the trilogy. In 'The Murders in the Rue Morgue', the main disturbing factor is the ape – although the sailor, with his 'sunburnt' appearance (p. 562) and his association with Malta (Maltese is a Semitic language) has certain 'alien' and hence threatening connotations, and is 'in some measure implicated' in the murders (p. 563). Before confronting the ape, Dupin has to eliminate various phantom opponents. The 'shrill voice' heard from the stairs is universally described by the witnesses as 'that *of a foreigner*' (p. 549) – a voice 'in whose *tones*, even, denizens of the five great divisions of Europe could recognize nothing familiar' (p. 550). It is thus implied that the murders could only have been committed by an alien, *unfamiliar* agent – that is, a non-European. Dupin suggests that 'it might have been the voice of an Asiatic – of an African' (p. 550), thus shifting responsibility for the murders to the cultural Other. The crime is thus alienated from the reader's world even before the agent is identified as non-human. Later, the narrator suggests another hypothesis: 'A madman . . . has done this deed – some raving maniac, escaped from a neighboring *Maison de Santé*' (p. 558). Here, the crime is attributed to an alien force within society – to the madman as exile within his own culture. The murders, then, are successively ascribed to the Other, whether without or within – to a 'savage' *alien*, or to someone mentally *alienated*. In fact, their author will prove to be more alien still – 'absolutely alien from humanity' (p. 558).

Repeated textual emphasis is placed on the non-human character of the murders, leading up to the identification of the ape (p. 559). Dupin describes them as 'altogether irreconcilable with our common notions of human action' (p. 557); the narrator declares, 'this is no *human* hair' (p. 558) and 'This . . . is the mark of no human hand' (p. 559). It is implied, then, that no human being could have committed the murders. Of course the text is lying; the murders are only a non-human act in degree (thanks to the ape's 'strength superhuman' – p. 558), not in kind. However, their ascription to an animal agent has a powerful ideological effect.

The ideology of criminality that 'The Murders in the Rue Morgue' produces is, in practice, the notion that crime is always committed by the Other – that there is *no continuity whatever* between the 'normal', 'respectable' citizen and the 'evil', 'sub-human' criminal – here represented symbolically by the ape. The use of an animal agent in the tale drives an ideological wedge between detective and criminal, seen as belonging quite literally to different *species*. Crime is thus robbed of a history and a discourse, and seen as the product of a self-referential, inexplicable, inhuman 'evil'.

However, this ideology of discontinuity is subverted in the letter of the text. Objectively, the incidence of the double theme – already noted above – tends to undermine any attempt to quarantine off the ape from the humans. First of all, the ape doubles the sailor – it imitates (apes) him. In accordance with what the text calls the 'imitative propensities' (p. 559) of its species, the ourang-outang is seen to copy the sailor's act of shaving (p. 565). The sailor's own relatively unrepressed sexuality, signified by his cudgel (p. 562), is doubled in extreme form by the ape's razor (stolen from him anyway), with its connotations of phallic sadism: 'so dangerous a weapon in the possession of an animal so ferocious' (p. 565). But, if the ape apes the sailor, Dupin apes the ape. The ourang-outang's 'imitative propensities' are doubled by Dupin's act of creating an artificial darkness (he is said to 'counterfeit' the night – p. 532). Later, just before identifying his adversary, he shows the narrator 'a little sketch I have here traced on this paper'. It is a *'fac-simile* drawing' of the ' "indentations of finger nails" ', upon the throat of Mademoiselle L'Espanaye' (pp. 558–9). Dupin thus doubles the ape by imitating its traces; he not only identifies it, but identifies *with* it (*'fac-simile'* implies that he *makes* himself *similar* to the ape). Further, at the end he doubles it again in the terms of his triumph over the Prefect: 'In his wisdom there is no *stamen*. It is all head and no body' (p. 568). By symbolically decapitating his rival, Dupin is following in the footsteps of the decapitator of Mme L'Espanaye (p. 538). The text thus effectively undermines its own ideology of 'normality', presenting detective and murderer as doubles (a latent criminal element in Dupin is implied in the verb 'counterfeit'). A certain *continuity* is established, in the teeth of the textual surface, between 'normal' and 'abnormal', 'civilised' and 'criminal'. At the end of 'The Murders in the Rue Morgue', the ape is caged in the zoo; yet the possibility remains that, sooner or later, Dupin himself might go ape!

The ideological divide between detective and criminal is maintained in 'The Mystery of Marie Rogêt', this time without significant subversion. Space does not permit a detailed analysis of the tale;[52] but it may be pointed out that here Dupin's opponents (potential and actual) are human, but still presented as Other. They include a gang of working-class marginals on whom suspicion at first rests, and the 'dark and swarthy' naval officer (p. 769) whom Dupin identifies as prime agent of Marie's death. The officer, ideologically suspect like the sailor of 'The Murders in the Rue Morgue' through his contact with other cultures, is seen as a 'wretch' ('Marie Rogêt', p. 771); the gang members are repeatedly labelled 'ruffians' and 'blackguards' (e.g. p. 757). This type of discourse tends to constitute the criminal as innately subhuman, belonging to a social universe alien to that of the 'respectable' detective (and reader).

The absence of any subversion of the 'normal'–'abnormal' divide in 'The Mystery of Marie Rogêt' may be related to the tale's relatively 'factual', documentary status. 'The Purloined Letter', however, marks a return to pure fiction; and in this text the antithesis between detective and criminal finally breaks down altogether.

The relation between Dupin and his opponent, the Minister D—, is here inserted into a textual structure of redoubled doubling. The purloined letter is itself double in various senses: it is front and back, inside and outside, deceptive reverse and authentic obverse. Indeed, as Henri Justin (1983) points out,[53] both literally and metaphorically, having been twice-folded on two different occasions – first by the Duke of S—, and then by D—.[54] It is, besides, twice doubled by substitutes – the 'somewhat similar' letter left by D— in the boudoir (p. 977), and the *'fac-simile'* left by Dupin in the hotel (p. 992). The characters, too, enter into relations of doubling; the narrator once again doubles Dupin, and places himself under the sign of doubling in the first sentence: 'I was enjoying the twofold luxury of meditation and a meerschaum' (p. 974) – thus making himself 'twofold', like the letter.[55] D— is doubled by his brother, and this doubling is itself signified in the context of 'letters' ('both have attained reputation in letters' – p. 986).

In Derrida's words, the text is a 'labyrinth of doubles';[56] and in this labyrinth Dupin and D— face each other as rivals. They are immediately signified as doubles on the plane of the letter (or grapheme) D, and by their respective relations to the purloined letter. Lacan's model of the two triangles, as specified above, places first D— and then Dupin in the position of the all-seeing look; the compulsion to repeat which Lacan finds at work in the text[57] determines doubling of minister by detective. Dupin repurloins the purloined letter, leaving a substitute *'fac-simile'*, to make which he has had to copy D—'s (disguised) handwriting and engage in the 'imitating' of the D— cipher (p. 992). The term *'fac-simile'* points back to Dupin's copy of the ape's traces in 'The Murders in the Rue Morgue'; in 'The Purloined Letter' too the detective, by imitating his opponent, risks becoming his facsimile.

Besides, Dupin and D— have other interchangeable characteristics. If D— is 'poet *and* mathematician' (p. 986), Dupin too disserts on mathematics (pp. 986–8) and says he is 'guilty of certain doggrel' (p. 979) ('guilty' implies a latent identification with the criminal). Both have unusually penetrating vision, and both are great literal readers and great metaphoric readers (of others' thoughts). In the message that Dupin leaves for D— inside the facsimile letter, the reference to Atreus and Thyestes (p. 993) introduces the theme of 'enemy brothers'; if, as the message implies, D— is Thyestes (who committed incest), then perhaps Dupin is his brother Atreus (who forced Thyestes to commit cannibalism) – in which case there would be little to choose between the two. Finally, as Lacan points out, both of them are 'feminised' by the letter;[58] D— feigns a 'diminutive and feminine' hand (p. 991), which Dupin in turn copies, and Dupin sees himself as a 'partisan' of the Queen (p. 993). Both, then, become identified with female subjects. It may be concluded that when Dupin declares, 'I knew him' (p. 988), it is a question not just of knowing one's enemy, but also of knowing one's double.

If, then, Dupin and D— are both double and doubled, and double each other, this structural characteristic of the text is in itself sufficient to subvert any attempt at constructing the detective as 'full' subject. Indeed, the question may be asked whether the two doubles do not become *interchangeable*. For Wilbur, they remain polarised, doubles but not equivalent; Dupin is seen as 'loftyminded', while D—, his 'unprincipled double', is 'base' and 'brutish'.[59] However, the text suggests that Dupin's motives are not so lofty or principled as Wilbur claims; certainly he comes over as less disinterested than in the other two tales. To the financial factor and competition with the Prefect are now added 'political prepossessions' and the desire for personal vengeance (p.993). Dupin does not emerge as any more or any less 'base' than his politically motivated, ambitious opponent.

It may even be legitimate to suggest that when Dupin calls D— 'that *monstrum horrendum*, an unprincipled man of genuis' (p. 993) the '*monstrum horrendum*' may perhaps be Dupin himself – that he is projecting his own unacceptable, 'monstrous' tendencies onto the minister. In 'The Murders in the Rue Morgue' the ape was Dupin's double, but not interchangeable with him; the species barrier assured that. In 'The Purloined Letter', however, the possibility is raised that the roles of hero and villain, 'principled' social saviour and 'unprincipled' conspirator, may have become exchangeable. Is Palmer's model of hero versus conspiracy maintained? Or does that antithesis break down? To answer these questions, both rival males must be placed in relation to the Queen, as representative of woman in the text.

As both the Bonaparte and Lacan readings referred to above suggest, 'The Purloined Letter' signifies female sexuality in unmistakably active terms. Lacan's notion of the 'feminising' effect of the letter suggests that it is, *inter alia*, a signifier of female desire. As is evident from the title, the text is centred on the letter, for Lacan 'the *true subject* of the tale'.[60] Its content is never revealed, although it is seen to be read twice – by the Queen (p. 977) and the Prefect (p. 983). D— has obviously read it, and the Prefect gives Dupin and the narrator a 'minute account' of its 'internal . . . appearance' (p. 981). It seems that every interested party has at least a general idea of its text, from its author, the Duke of S—, to the last purloiner, Dupin – except for the King (who is unaware of its existence) and the reader! The letter, as micro-text, is endlessly signified in the macro-text, but never quoted or paraphrased; its inside forms a gaping hole at the heart of the text. It may be concluded that its text must contain subversive material, constituting a symbolic threat to the cultural order.

As Lacan suggests, the purloined letter may be either a 'love letter' or a 'conspiratorial letter'.[61] In either instance (or both), it places the Queen in a position of insubordination towards her husband and overlord: 'this letter is the symbol of a pact and . . . , even if its addressee does not act on that pact, the letter's existence places her in a symbolic chain alien to the chain that constitutes her loyalty'.[62] By entering on a pact (even if only latent) with S—, the Queen is affirming herself as active woman, and thus breaking the *cultural* law; at the same time, the letter makes her an actual or potential conspirator against the *juridical* law – a second Guinevere, guilty, in Lacan's words, of *'high treason'*.[63]

If, then, the letter signifies – to use Derrida's phrase – 'the Queen's desire',[64] then the court scandal that threatens to break conceals the greater scandal of female dissent. The silenced discourse of the letter is the discourse of female sexuality, that if spoken would undermine the patriarchal order. Both Dupin and D—, as privileged males, identify with that order; yet their strategies for the defence of that order divide them.

D—'s strategy is essentially that of exposure. If the letter were shown to the King, then, as Lacan suggests, a 'Chambre Ardente' could await the Queen;[65] divorce or execution could follow. D— can, of course, either sell the letter back to the Queen or show it to the King; but, as long as he possesses it, the threat of exposure hangs over her, and her 'honor and peace are . . . jeopardized' (p. 976). D—'s hold on the letter thus maintains the possibility of the public denunciation and punishment of female desire. Dupin's strategy, in contrast, implies the private acceptance and public cover-up of active femaleness. His aim is not to denounce the Queen, but to retrieve the letter and silence its content. Women, it seems, can have desires so long as the public does not know; this aim is achieved in 'The Purloined Letter', in so far as the reader (representative of the public) is denied access to the letter's text!

Dupin's position towards the letter implies, in practice, a certain *solidarity with woman*; his strategy is more 'liberal' than the minister's, since, however hypocritical, it permits a certain (discreet) freedom for female desire. In spite of his conservatism, Dupin has been forced by the letter to identify with an oppressed social group! In this sense, indeed, the letter has a 'feminising' effect. It is necessary, however, to distinguish between the ways in which the letter 'feminises' Dupin and D— respectively. If it enlists Dupin as a 'partisan' of the Queen, its loss devalues D— in relation to her. Its return will allow her, at some later date, to 'defy' the minister's blackmail: 'For eighteen months the Minister has had her in his power. She has now him in hers' (p. 993). In this context, Lacan is correct to claim that 'the Minister comes to be castrated',[66] since the 'normal' male–female power relation is reversed.

From all the above, the surprising conclusion may be drawn that perhaps the real conspirator is not so much D— as Dupin himself. Dupin is part of a conspiracy of silence over the letter; he defeats D—'s conspiracy against the Queen, but at the cost of tacitly assenting to the Queen's conspiracy with S— against the King. It is thus doubtful whether Dupin can be seen in 'The Purloined Letter' as the saviour of the existing order – especially as his action reverses the power relation between Queen and minister, woman and man. Indeed, D— himself can be seen as the legitimate defender of patriarchal culture, since his strategy implies the putting of woman 'back in her place'. The roles of hero and villain, conspirator and social saviour, have in 'The Purloined Letter' become interchangeable; both Dupin and D— can be placed in either role. At this point, the detective–thriller genre may be said to have broken down.

The Dupin trilogy *may*, of course, be read *à la* Derrida as a series of labyrinths, a hall of mirrors in which one signifier doubles and distorts another in an infinite regression of self-destroying structures.[67] However, rather than deconstructing the texts out of history, materialist criticism can place them as productions of a historically specific ideology: the detective as 'full' subject, guarantor of the social order, and exponent of competitive individualism and 'disinterested' science. The textual structure of doubling, rather than, as Derrida would have it, prising the texts away from *any* specific meaning or 'truth',[68] serves to undermine the ideological model of the subject that they construct, and thus to expose the limits of that ideology.[69] If Poe wrote no more detective stories after 1844,[70] the reason may lie in the breakdown, in 'The Purloined Letter', of the 'normal'–'abnormal', 'civilised'–'criminal' antithesis constructed in the earlier tales. The abandonment of empiricism; the interchangeability between hero and conspirator; the disturbing insistence of female desire: all these factors lead to the disintegration of the generic structure constructed in 'The Murders in the Rue Morgue'. If the inventor of the detective story stopped writing in the genre, it may have been because the genre had come to disintegrate under his own pen.

Notes

1. The text used is that of *The Collected Works of Edgar Allan Poe*, ed.
    T. O. Mabbott, 3 vols (Cambridge, Mass.: Harvard University
    Press, 1969–78) ii, 527–68 ('The Murders in the Rue Morgue'), iii,
    723–74 ('The Mystery of Marie Rogêt') and iii, 974–93 ('The
    Purloined Letter'). Page references are given in the text (vols ii and
    iii are continuously paginated).
2. Arthur Conan Doyle, quoted in Brander Matthews, 'Poe and the
    Detective Story', *Scribner's Magazine*, Sep 1907; repr. in Eric W.
    Carlson (ed.), *The Recognition of Edgar Allan Poe: Selected Criticism
    since 1829* (Ann Arbor: University of Michigan Press, 1966) pp. 82–
    94 (quoting from p. 90).
3. Paul Valéry, 'Situation de Baudelaire' (11928), in *Oeuvres*, i (Paris:
    Gallimard [Bibliothèque de la Pléiade], 1957) 598–613 (see
    p. 606).
4. Walter Benjamin, 'The Paris of the Second Empire in Baudelaire'
    (1938), in Benjamin, *Charles Baudelaire: A Lyric Poet in the Era of High
    Capitalism*, tr. H. Zohn (London: New Left Books, 1973) pp. 11–106
    (see p. 43).
5. T. S. Eliot, 'From Poe to Valéry', *Hudson Review*, Autumn 1949; repr.
    in Carlson, *Recognition*, pp. 205–19 (see p. 208).
6. Jorge Luis Borges, 'El poeta del regreso', *Cambio 16* (Madrid), 440 (11
    May 1980) 131. (NB. All quotations from texts written in languages
    other than English are in my own translation, unless otherwise
    specified; but page references are to the original).
7. Howard Haycraft, *Murder for Pleasure: The Life and Times of the
    Detective Story* (New York: Appleton-Century, 1941) p. 11.
8. Julian Symons, *Mortal Consequences: A History from the Detective Story
    to the Crime Novel* (New York: Schocken Books, 1973) p. 27.
9. Jerry Palmer, *Thrillers: Genesis and Structure of a Popular Genre*
    (London: Edward Arnold, 1978) p. 107.
10. Cf. also William Godwin, *Caleb Williams* (1794); E. T. A. Hoffman,
    'Mademoiselle de Scudéry' (1819); Charles Dickens, *Barnaby Rudge*
    (1840), *Bleak House* (1853); Wilkie Collins, *The Moonstone* (1868).
11. Terry Eagleton, 'Capitalism, Modernism and Postmodernism', *New
    Left Review*, 152 (July–Aug 1985) 60–73 (quoting from p. 71).
12. Richard Wilbur, 'The Poe Mystery Case', *New York Review of Books*,
    13 July 1967, pp. 25–8 (quoting from p. 27). Cf. the reading of E. H.
    Davidson, in *Poe: A Critical Study* (Cambridge, Mass.: Harvard
    University Press, 1957) pp. 213–22.
13. Jacques Lacan, 'Le Séminaire sur "La Lettre volée"' (1957), in *Ecrits*,
    i (Paris: Seuil [Collection Points], 1970) 19–53; Jacques Derrida, 'Le
    Factuer de la vérité', *Poétique*, 21 (1975) 96–147.
14. Marie Bonaparte, *Edgar Poe: étude psychanalytique* (1933), tr. J. Rodker as
    The Life and Works of Edgar Allan Poe: A Psychoanalytic Interpretation
    (London: Hogarth Press, 1949; repr. New York: Humanities Press,
    1971) pp. 447–54. Cf. Sigmund Freud, 'On the Sexual Theories of
    Children' (1908), in *Pelican Freud Library*, vii: *On Sexuality* (Har-
    mondsworth: Penguin, 1977) pp. 187–204.

15. Bonaparte, *Poe*, p. 483.
16. The Lacan–Bonaparte relationship is pointed out by Derrida, in *Poétique*, 21, pp. 115–16.
17. Lacan, *Ecrits*, I, 47.
18. Ibid., p. 20.
19. See Derrida, in *Poétique*, 21, p. 123; cf. Sigmund Freud, 'The "Uncanny"' (1919), in *Pelican Freud Library*, XIV: *Art and Literature* (Harmondsworth: Penguin, 1985) pp. 339–76, esp. pp. 356–8.
20. Derrida, in *Poétique*, 21, p. 138.
21. Stephen Knight, *Form and Ideology in Crime Fiction* (London: Macmillan, 1980) p. 39.
22. Palmer, *Thrillers*, p. 148.
23. Ibid., p. 203.
24. Ibid., p. 87.
25. Ibid., p. 66.
26. Ibid., p. 22–3.
27. Ibid., p. 101.
28. Ibid., p. 23.
29. Ibid., p. 64.
30. Ibid., pp. 153–80.
31. Ibid., pp. 181–201.
32. See Ibid., pp. 7–16.
33. Lacan, *Ecrits*, I, 24.
34. Cf. Roland Barthes, 'Introduction à l'analyse structurale des récits' (1966), repr. in G. Genette and T. Todorov (eds), *Poétique du récit* (Paris: Seuil [Collection Points], 1977) pp. 7–57, esp. p. 15; S. L. P. Bellei, '"The Purloined Letter": A Theory of Perception', *Poe Studies*, 9, no. 2 (Dec 1976) 40–2.
35. Mireille Vincent, 'Le Grand singe fauve', *Delta* (Montpellier), 1 (1975) 67–82 (quoting from p. 68).
36. See Derrida, in *Poétique*, 21, p. 137; Wilbur, in *New York Review of Books*, 13 July 1967, p. 27; J. A. L. Lemay, 'The Psychology of "The Murders in the Rue Morgue"', *American Literature*, 54 (May 1982) 165–88, esp. p. 170.
37. See Knight, *Form and Ideology*, p. 42.
38. Such a view is argued in D. B. Stauffer, 'Poe as Phrenologist: The Example of Monsieur Dupin', in R. P. Veler (ed.), *Papers on Poe* (Springfield, Ohio: Chantry Music Press, 1972) pp. 113–25.
39. See Raymond Williams, *Keywords: A Vocabulary of Culture and Society* (London: Fontana, 1976) p. 234.
40. Ibid., p. 235.
41. For this concept, see Boaventura de Sousa Santos, 'Da sociologia da ciência à política científica', *Revista crítica de ciências sociais* (Coimbra) 1 (June 1978) 11–56, which contains a critique of Robert Merton, *Science and Democratic Social Order* (1942).
42. P. B. Shelley, 'A Defence of Poetry' (1821), in *Selected Poetry, Prose and Letters* (London: Nonesuch Press, 1951) pp. 1023–55 (quoting from p. 1032).
43. John Keats, letter to R. Woodhouse (27 Oct 1818), in M. B. Forman

(ed.), *The Letters of John Keats* (London: Oxford University Press, 1952) pp. 226–8.

44. Knight, *Form and Ideology*, p. 60.
45. See Ferdinand de Saussure, *Cours de linguistique générale* (1916), tr. W. Baskin as *Course in General Linguistics* (London: Fontana, 1974) pp. 122–7; Jonathan Culler, Introduction to this edition, p. xx.
46. George Lukács, *History and Class Consciousness* (1923), tr. R. Livingstone (London: Merlin, 1971) p. 6.
47. Ibid., p. 8.
48. Ibid., p. 3.
49. See Knight, *Form and Ideology*, p. 40.
50. Cf. Lukács, *Studies in European Realism* (1948), tr. E. Bone (London: Hillway, 1950) pp. 47–64; Raymond Williams, *Culture and Society 1780–1950* (Harmondsworth: Penguin, 1958) pp. 30–48.
51. Arthur Conan Doyle, 'The Greek Interpreter' (*Memoirs of Sherlock Holmes*, 1894), in *The Penguin Complete Sherlock Holmes* (Harmondsworth: Penguin, 1981) p. 435.
52. For the relation between the tale and the historical murder of Mary Cecilia Rogers, see W. K. Wimsatt, Jr, 'Poe and the Mystery of Mary Rogers', *PMLA*, 56 (1941) 230–48; T. O. Mabbott, in Poe, *Works*, III, 715–22.
53. Henri Justin, 'The Fold is the Thing: Poe Criticism in France in the Last Five Years', *Poe Studies*, 16, no. 2 (Dec 1983) 25–31 (see p. 25).
54. Mabbott points out that 'the letter was on an old-fashioned four-page sheet, with text on the first and address on the last page, and so could be turned inside out' (Poe, *Works*, III, 996n).
55. Cf. Justin, in *Poe Studies*, 16, no. 2, p. 25.
56. Derrida, in *Poétique*, 21, p. 138.
57. See Lacan, *Ecrits*, I, 19–25; cf. Sigmund Freud, *Beyond the Pleasure Principle* (1920), in *Pelican Freud Library*, XI: *On Metapsychology: The Theory of Psychoanalysis* (Harmondsworth: Penguin, 1984) pp. 275–338, esp. pp. 288–94.
58. See Lacan, *Ecrits*, I, 46–51.
59. Wilbur, in *New York Review of Books*, 13 July 1967, pp. 25–6.
60. Lacan, *Ecrits*, I, 40.
61. Ibid., p. 38.
62. Ibid.
63. Ibid.
64. Derrida, in *Poétique*, 21, p. 121.
65. Lacan, *Ecrits*, I, 43.
66. Lacan, 'Présentation', in *Ecrits*, I, 7–12 (quoting from p. 8).
67. Cf. Derrida, in *Poétique*, 21, p. 138.
68. See ibid., pp. 103–4.
69. Cf. Pierre Macherey, *Pour une théorie de la production littéraire* (1966), tr. G. Wall as *A Theory of Literary Production* (London: Routledge and Kegan Paul, 1978) pp. 61–6.
70. 'Thou Art the Man' (1844), which Mabbott places just after 'The Purloined Letter' (Poe, *Works*, III, 1043), is best viewed as a self parodic text.

3

Camera Eye/Private Eye

PETER HUMM

In *Farewell, My Lovely*, Raymond Chandler refers to 'a Baltimore detective with a camera eye as rare as a pink zebra'.[1] What I want to do in this essay is to show that, however rare such a man may have been in Baltimore, he is a characteristic and significant hero, not only for the thriller writers of the 1930s and 1940s, but also for those other writers concerned to provide some kind of witness to what Christopher Isherwood called the 'fantastic realities' of the time.[2] This will mean moving beyond Baltimore and the canon of American crime fiction in order to register the appearance of this figure on both sides of the Atlantic and in a variety of cultural forms. This essay, then, tries to place some popular fictions in a cultural context defined through the simultaneous sighting of a metaphor – the 'camera eye' which appears in the fiction, the journalism and the films, as well as the photographic record, of the period. Breaking the bounds of this book's title becomes a way to expand the notions of genre and formula that have shadowed the investigation of crime fiction.

The classic statement of the writer as witness comes from Christopher Isherwood's *Goodbye to Berlin*: 'I am a camera with its shutter open, quite passive, recording, not thinking. Recording the man shaving at the window opposite and the woman in the kimono washing her hair. Some day, all this will have to be developed, carefully printed, fixed.'[3] What is important here is the exactness of Isherwood's metaphor in describing the *process* of photography. The slow, comma'd sentences mark the stage-by-stage ritual of photographic procedure in the years before Polaroids or one-hour fotomats. There is no instant button or formula to cut short the necessary delays between recording and thinking, between witnessing the scene in Berlin and that future day when all this will have to be developed and made permanent. The Christopher who appears as a witness to life in the streets and cafés of Berlin is thereby separated from Christopher Isherwood, the author: he is made a function, a 'convenient ventriloquist's dummy', as Isherwood calls him in the introduction; a camera eye. In this way, Isherwood both guarantees the accuracy of what is being recorded and leaves undecided, undeveloped the full meaning of what the camera sees.

This formulation of Isherwood's – the fantastic realities of the everyday world leading the writer to place recording before thinking – corresponds closely to something that the American poet Wallace Stevens said in explaining his own attempts to respond to the quickening social concerns of the thirties. Stevens felt that the Depression and threatening war had moved everyone's attention 'in the direction of reality, that is to say, in the direction of fact', and he was convinced that this response was right, that 'in the presence of extraordinary actuality, consciousness takes the place of the imagination'.[4] This is an important statement because it points to the cause and the effect of the new direction that many writers were to take in the thirties, and particularly to the new concern, in both America and Britain, with forms of documentary and reportage.

Just as Wallace Stevens and Christopher Isherwood come to a similar theoretical position, so, on both sides of the Atlantic, there are significant equivalents in cultural practice. The Living Newspapers of the Federal Theater are close in style and ideology, as well as in name, to the Living Newspapers produced in the same years by the Unity Theatre in London. The writers and artists attached to such New Deal agencies as the Works Progress Administration and the Farm Security Administration – Saul Bellow, Jackson Pollock, Aaron Copland, Walker Evans – find their equivalent in Humphrey Jennings, John Grierson, Benjamin Britten, W. H. Auden and others who worked for the General Post Office Film Unit. There was, in these years immediately before the war, an organised act of witness recorded not only in individual novels and films but also, more typically, in the state guides produced by the Federal Writers Project and in the frequent reports published by Mass Observation. The name of this organisation, founded in 1937 to respond to the 'urgency of fact, the voicelessness of everyman [by] studying the every day lives and feelings of ordinary people' reinforces the changing interpretation of consciousness'.[5] The term was to be used not in the modernist sense of an introspective withdrawal into the psychological stream but in a more urgent, in some ways more primitive, sense: consciousness was now concentrated on confronting and documenting the immediacy of the everyday world.

The anxiety to observe and record rather than imagine can be seen at its most engagingly primitive in the prospectus that Henry Luce, the founder of *Time* magazine, produced for his new publication *Life*:

> To see life; to see the world; to eyewitness great events; to watch the faces of the poor and the gestures of the proud; to see strange things – machines, armies, multitudes . . . to see things a thousand miles away; things hidden behind walls and within rooms, things dangerous to come to, the women that men love and many children; to see and to take pleasure in seeing; to see and be amazed; to see and be instructed.[6]

This ideal was to be accomplished not by the simple haphazard printing of photographs but by a new collaboration between writer and photographer, by what Luce called the 'mind-guided camera', which could 'harness the main stream of optical consciousness of our time'.[7]

One simple reason for the increased awareness of the camera as a technical model among writers at this time was that so many of them, particularly in America, had experience of exactly this kind of collaboration. John Steinbeck toured the Okie camps in California with *Life* photographer Horace Bristol, planning a *Life* article and an illustrated documentary book on the conditions they had found there. He decided, however, to use this material not in his journalism but for a novel. But, when *The Grapes of Wrath* was published in 1939, *Life* still managed to share the credit by boasting that 'never before had the facts behind a great work of fiction been so carefully researched by the news camera'.[8] Two years earlier, Erskine Caldwell and the photographer Margaret Bourke White had travelled through the South to produce a documentary book with the exemplary thirties title *You Have Seen Their Faces*. But the most persuasive collaboration between photography and prose, and an essential document in understanding the relation between consciousness and imagination, is Walker Evans and James Agee's *Let Us Now Praise Famous Men*.

This too began as a commission for a Henry Luce publication; this time it was *Fortune* magazine, which sent Agee and Evans to spend July and August 1936 with the families of three white tenant farmers in Alabama. *Fortune* turned down the article, and Agee's revised and expanded text and Evans's photographs were not finally published until 1941. In the Preface, Agee explains that

> The nominal subject is North American cotton tenantry as examined in the daily living of three representative white tenant families. Actually, the effort is to recognize the stature of a portion of unimagined existence and to contrive techniques proper to its recording, communication, analysis and defense. The immediate instruments are two: the motionless camera and the printed word. The governing instrument which is also one of the centers of the subject, is individual anti-authoritative human consciousness.[9]

Throughout the book, Agee strains to define the privacy of that individual consciousness in perceiving 'the aesthetic reality within the actual world'.[10] 'Consciousness,' he argues, 'is shifted from the imagined, the revisive to the effort to perceive simply the cruel radiance of what is.' He continues,

> This is why the camera seems to me, next to unassisted and weaponless consciousness, the central instrument of our time; and is why I in turn feel such rage at its misuse, which has spread so nearly a universal corruption of sight that I know of less than a dozen alive whose eyes I can trust even as much as my own.[11]

What alarmed the editors of *Fortune* was not just the angry insistence of Agee's prose but the exhaustive seriousness with which he and Walker Evans took the practice of documentary. The central section of *Let Us Now Praise Famous Men* is a 50,000 word inventory listing and describing the contents of the families' houses down to the grain of the floorboards and the rust in a metal dipper. The whole book represents an intense effort of perception, as in description Agee gives of himself, 'late in a summer night . . . looking at a lighted coal oil lamp'.

Agee writes three paragraphs describing the glass of the base and bowl, the feel of the oil between his finger and thumb and the 'subtle sweating of this oil' on the surface of the lamp. 'I do not understand nor try to deduce this, but I like it; I run my thumb upon it and smell of my thumb, and smooth away its streaked print on the glass; and I wipe my thumb and forefinger dry against my pants, and keep on looking.'[12] Agee keeps on looking because he is concerned to 'convey some single thing as nearly as possible as that thing is'.[13] He wants, as he says on the final page of the book, to give these matters 'extreme clearness and edge and honor'.

A very similar ambition runs through another classic documentary of the thirties – Ernest Hemingway's *Death in the Afternoon*. Like James Agee and Walker Evans, Hemingway moves between a documentary account of a particular world – here bull-fighting – and an intense examination of his own moral and aesthetic relation to that world. What is special to Hemingway is the need to confront a world of violence and death:

> I was trying to write then and I found the greatest difficulty ... was to put down what really happened in action; what the actual things were which produced the emotion that you experienced. ... I was trying to learn to write, commencing with the simplest things, and one of the simplest things of all and the most fundamental is violent death. ... I had read many books in which, when the author tried to convey it, he only produced a blur, and I decided that this was because either the author had never seen it clearly or at the moment of it, he had physically or mentally shut his eyes. ... If these very simple things were to be made permanent ... it could not be done with any shutting of the eyes.[14]

Death in the Afternoon serves, then, to connect the particular way of seeing that I have been describing, with a world of action and violent death. It is in this documentary on the craft of the bull-fighter and the writer, as much as in stories such as 'The Killers', that Hemingway suggests his own affinity with the code of the private eye. Hemingway's refusal to shut his eyes to violence is represented as heroic and yet, as his parodied appearance as a mean-spoken cop in *Farewell, My Lovely* suggests, there is an unnerving blankness in that stare. Before finally discussing the documentary vision of Raymond Chandler and Dashiell Hammett, I want to consider the sinister appearance of this photographic motif in some of the best-known thrillers of the period. Again, I am not staying within America, although in my first example, the opening scene of Graham Greene's *A Gun for Sale*, there is a very

conscious reference to the tradition of the American thriller. As his
title and his choice of criminal hero suggest, Greene was a long
way from the guilty vicarage.

Raven is a mercenary hired to assassinate a socialist minister; he
is also a killer with a camera eye. 'His eyes, like little concealed
cameras, photographed the room instantaneously: the desk, the
easy chair, the map on the wall, the door to the bedroom behind,
the wide window above the bright, cold Christmas street.'[15] After
Raven has killed the minister and shot the secretary,

> He opened the bedroom door; his eyes again photographed
> the scene, the single bed, the wooden chair, the dusty chest of
> drawers, a photograph of a young Jew with a small scar on his
> chin as if he had been struck there with a club, a pair of brown
> wooden hairbrushes initialled J. K., everywhere cigarette ash;
> the home of an old untidy man; the home of the Minister for
> War.[16]

Raven makes sure of the secretary by shooting her 'with the
automatic almost touching her eyes' and leaves the job.

Greene uses the camera eye in much the same way as Hemingway stares at the scene. There is the same photographic registering
of detail, the same determination not to discriminate between the
banal and the significant. But, where Hemingway conveys the
even detachment of an eyewitness, Greene varies the pace of the
scene: the passive, unblinking calm of Raven's camera eye frames
the extreme violence of his actions. In this cinematic way, Greene
establishes the controlled mechanical efficiency of a professional
killer, whose pride it is that 'he wasn't a man who imagined things;
he knew'.[17]

There is a similar opposition between knowing–recording and
and the dangerous uncertainties of imagination in *Brighton Rock*,
another of Greene's novels which is focused through the criminal
rather than the weary detective. Pinkie, with his 'grey inhuman
seventeen year old eyes', eyes like 'those of an old man in whom
human feeling has died' dreads the pull of the imagination.[18] 'The
imagination hadn't awoken. That was his strength. He couldn't see
through other people's eyes or feel with their nerves.'[19]

One last example of the cold-eyed killer comes from another
novel which proves the vulnerability of distinctions between
popular and canonic literature: William Faulkner's *Sanctuary*.

Again, the opening scene shows the confrontation between the gangster – here given the emblematic name of Popeye – and the civilian:

> From beyond the screen of bushes which surrounded the spring, Popeye watched the man drinking. . . . Popeye watched the man – a tall, thin, man, hatless in worn grey flannel trousers and carrying a tweed coat over his arm – emerge from the path and kneel to drink from the spring. . . .
>
> Across the spring Popeye appeared to contemplate him with two knobs of black rubber. 'I'm asking you', Popeye said, 'what's that in your pocket?' . . .
>
> Popeye's eyes looked like rubber knobs, like they'd give to the touch and then recover with the whorled smudge of the thumb on them.
>
> 'I want to reach Jefferson before dark', Benbow said. 'You can't keep me here like this.'
>
> Without removing the cigarette Popeye spat part of it into the spring.
>
> 'You can't stop me like this', Benbow said. 'Suppose I break and run.'
>
> Popeye put his eyes on Benbow, like rubber. 'Do you want to run?'
>
> 'No,' Benbow said.
>
> Popeye removed his eyes. 'Well, don't, then.'[20]

What this coincidence suggests is that Greene and Faulkner extend the logic of the camera eye to provide an underworld, subversive commentary on that balance of consciousness against imagination. Raven, Pinkie and especially Popeye are reduced, as they reduce others, to the external. Popeye, with his tight black suit, slanted hat and cigarette, is a cartoon gangster, an artificial figure, 'bloodless, as though seen by electric light'.[21] His face is a mechanical replica that misses humanity; it has 'that vicious depthless quality of stamped tin'.[22] Even at their most violent, these figures remain mechanically distant and uninvolved, using objects to hold off the reality of others. When Raven almost touches the minister's old and helpless secretary, it is with his automatic; when Popeye rapes Temple, it is with a corn cob.

In choosing the genre of the thriller, Greene and Faulkner have also chosen to sour its conventional heroisms. Their focus on the narrowing calculations of the criminal's vision is a double-edged commentary on the use that could be made of the limitations of the formula they were working within. The inhuman eyes of Pinkie or Popeye unsettle both the classical detective's reliance on reason as the corrective to a disordered world and the private eye's steady observation. Their depthless gaze forces a recognition of the dangerous reduction of evil to the parlour-game formalities of England or the street heroics of America. In translating the thriller to the rural South or to the back streets of Brighton, Faulkner and Greene do more than change expected places; their use of a popular genre becomes a dislocating critique both of the convention and of the criminal world it describes.

Sinda Gregory has shown in her study of Dashiell Hammett how the 'rules that classical detective writers like Chesterton formulated can be almost completely re-written to fit the hard-boiled story'.[23] The principles that G. K. Chesterton listed in 'How to Write a Detective Story' – the story must illuminate not obscure, be simple not complex, be bound to the 'rules of both common sense and artistic consistency' – are reversed in the dark tradition of *Black Mask* and the Hollywood *film noir*.[24] Where a detective in the English or Anglophile tradition can rely on everybody staying clearly in place on the Cluedo board, the private eye has to confront a world, which is always shifting. He has both to keep up with the action and make what sense of it he can. This is made the more testing because the private eye, unlike the amateur scientist with the magnifying glass, is himself directly, often brutally, involved with the world of violence he is hired to investigate – as Hammett's Continental Op explains in *Red Harvest* to a woman who wants something more 'scientific' than his vague plan to 'stir things up' to see what will happen:

> 'So that's the way you scientific detectives work. My God! for a fat, middle-aged, hard-boiled, pig-headed guy, you've got the vaguest way of doing things I ever heard of'.
> 'Plans are all right sometimes', I said. 'And sometimes just stirring things up is all right – if you're tough enough to survive, and keep your eyes open so you'll see what you want when it comes to the top.'[25]

The private eye, then, moves continually between action and direct observation; he is never allowed the breathing-space of anticipation or interpretation. This existential insistence upon the unrelenting present is what gives the hard-boiled detective story its immediacy and force. What distinguishes the work of Dashiell Hammett and Raymond Chandler is their ability to write with the 'objectivity, economy, restraint' that Joseph Shaw, the editor of *Black Mask*, demanded, and, at the same time, to question the effect of this detachment upon their heroes and on the world in which they operated.[26]

This is the description the Continental Op gives of the woman who later criticises him for doing no more than keeping his eyes open:

> The young woman got up, kicked a couple of newspapers out of her way, and came to me with one hand out. She was an inch or two taller than I, which made her about five feet eight. She had a broad-shouldered, full-breasted, round-hipped body and big muscular legs. The hand she gave me was soft, warm, strong. Her face was the face of a girl of twenty-five already showing signs of wear. Little lines crossed the corners of her big ripe mouth. Fainter lines were beginning to make nets around her thick-lashed eyes. They were large eyes, blue and a bit bloodshot.
>
> Her coarse hair – brown – needed trimming and was parted crookedly. One side of her upper lip had been rouged higher than the other. Her dress was of a particularly unbecoming wine colour, and it gaped here and there down one side, where she had neglected to snap the fasteners or they had popped open. There was a run down the front of her left stocking.
>
> This was the Dinah Brand who took her pick of Poisonville's men, according to what I had been told.[27]

The closing gibe reveals the Op's contempt for the gap between what he is told by others and what he can see for himself, but the ungiving meanness of his own description also reveals an objectivity that denies any human sympathy. Our unease is reinforced when the Op repeats the same remorseless detail in his final description of Dinah Brand.

> I opened my eyes in the dull light of morning sun filtering through drawn blinds.
>
> I was lying face down on the dining room floor, my head

resting on my left forearm. My right arm was stretched straight
out. My right hand held the round blue and white handle of
Dinah Brand's ice pick. The pick's six inch needle-sharp blade
was buried in Dinah Brand's left breast.

    She was lying on her back, dead. Her long muscular legs were
stretched out toward the kitchen door. There was a run down
the front of her right stocking.[28]

The Op is so distanced from the scene he outlines that he treats not
only Dinah Brand's body but also his own as an object in a
diagram. The Op's recourse to the automatic language of the
forensic witness marks Hammett's own distance from the professional detachment he once shared. Hammett's reasons for
leaving the Pinkerton Detective Agency are still not clear, but his
criticism of the deadening impersonality it forced upon its operat-
ives is as important as his respect for their hard independence.

    The Continental Op is a famously anonymous hero, but, when
Hammett gives his private eye a name and full physical description, he continues to keep his readers at a distance by moving to
third-person narration. *The Maltese Falcon* begins with a description
of Sam Spade that places him as coldly on the slab as the post-
mortemed Dinah Brand. His face is reduced to a motif, his body
exposed to the photographic glare of Hammett's prose.

    Samuel Spade's jaw was long and bony, his chin a jutting V
under the more flexible V of his mouth. His nostrils curved back
to make another small V. His yellow-grey eyes were horizontal.
The V motif was picked up again, by thickish brows vising
outward from twin creases above a hooked nose, and his pale
brown hair grew down – from high flat temples – in a point on
his forehead.[29] He took off his pajamas. The smooth thickness of
his arms, legs, and body, the sag of his big rounded shoulders,
made his body like a bear's. It was like a shaved bear's: his chest
was hairless. His skin was childishly soft and pink.[30]

The Op functions like a voice-over, invisible but insistent; Sam
Spade is fully described but never explained. The longer the
description, the more incongruous it seems, with the lupine head
upon the pink bear shoulders. The camera eye of the Op, like the
camera eye turned on Sam Spade, reveals that careful objective
description is not enough: an alert consciousness must be balanced

by a sympathetic imagination. Even then, when the case is over, the mystery of individual motivation remains. Moving between the objective voice of an anonymous narrator and his puzzling close-up on Sam Spade, Hammett separates himself from any simple reliance upon a hero or narrator, who is no more than an eye.

Hammett's five novels, written within a five-year period, range over contrasting styles of mystery and have two other investigators in Ned Beaumont and Nick Charles. Raymond Chandler's career was longer but stayed more closely attached to a private-eye hero, whose personality was tended with an affection that Hammett's detachment would never allow. And yet, despite or perhaps because of his sentiment towards Philip Marlowe, Chandler fretted against the limitations of formula fiction. Describing his own apprenticeship with *Black Mask* he wrote, 'some of us tried pretty hard to break out of the forumula but we usually got caught and sent back. To exceed the limits of a formula without destroying it is the dream of every magazine writer who is not a hopeless hack.'[31] Later, he made a more careful distinction: 'my whole career is based on the idea that the formula doesn't matter, the thing that counts is what you do with the formula; that is to say, it is a matter of style'.[32]

That tension between the demands of formula and the expression of a style is maintained throughout Chandler's writing. What Chandler gained from the discipline of genre writing was an 'objective method' by which he felt able to 'render a state of mind ... purely through the tone of the description'.[33] Where Hammett had made the camera eye of his narrator condemning evidence of the dangers of objectivity, Chandler used the technique to present the competing claims of consciousness and imagination. Through his narrator, Chandler manages to combine a photographically vivid description with a sense of individual personality; he moves at exactly the right moment from the camera eye to the human eye and imagination of Philip Marlowe. A famous example of Chandler's method is the description of Moose Malloy in the opening chapter of *Farewell, My Lovely*:

> He was a big man but not more than six feet five inches tall and not wider than a beer truck. He was about ten feet away from me. His arms hung loose at his sides and a forgotten cigar smoked behind his enormous fingers. Slim quiet negroes passed up and down the street and stared at him with darting side

glances. He was worth looking at. He wore a shaggy borsalino hat, a rough grey sports coat with white golf balls on it for buttons, a brown shirt, a yellow tie, pleated grey flannel slacks and alligator shoes with white explosions on the toes. From his outer breast pocket cascaded a show handkerchief of the same brilliant yellow as his tie. There were a couple of coloured feathers tucked into the band of his hat, but he didn't really need them. Even on Central Avenue, not the quietest dressed street in the world, he looked about as inconspicuous as a tarantula on a slice of angel food.[34]

It's that last line, the wisecracking simile of the tarantula on a slice of angel food, that is so characteristic of Chandler's writing and that enables him to make Philip Marlowe's consciousness, in James Agee's phrase, the subject as well as the governing instrument of each book.

Like Agee, like Isherwood, like Hemingway, Chandler insists that the force of the objective, documentary vision is that it stems from an intensely personal effort of perception. While Chandler claimed that the purpose of the simile is 'to convey at once a simple visual image', his best lines tell us as much about the imagination which created them as they do about what they describe. Moose Malloy is certainly worth looking at, but it is Marlowe's descriptive wit that we finally remember. That parting shot switches control of the scene, not just to Marlowe's point of view, but to the ironic, self-conscious imagination that directs his perception of the world. Metaphor is the private eye's best defence against a world which is always threatening to sap him unconscious.

Raymond Chandler made only one attempt at adapting one of his own novels for the screen. After several months work, he handed over the script of *The Lady in the Lake* to another writer and refused a screen credit. The film is famous now not for its writing but for the elaborate camera-eye technique employed by the actor–director Robert Montgomery. Marlowe is played by the voice (and occasional reflected image) of Robert Montgomery and by the lens of the camera, so that the viewer becomes the detective. The effect of this audience identification with the camera is a ponderous return to the puzzle format of the parlour detective fiction Chandler so disliked. The audience is told at the beginning: You'll see it as I saw it. You'll meet the people; you'll find the clues. And maybe you'll solve it quick and maybe you won't.[35] And with that jocular warning, all tension and personality disappear and we are left with the mechanical solution of a technical problem. Chandler knew that the camera eye by itself was not enough; recording the facts, getting the picture is what the cops do. As one explains to Marlowe in chapter 14 of *The Lady in the Lake*, 'We don't think anything at all. What we do is investigate and find out.'[36] What Marlowe does, what the private eye must do, is to go beyond this to make sure that the image recorded by the camera eye is finally developed, carefully printed, fixed.

Chandler once distinguished between 'two kinds of writers; writers who write stories and writers who write writing',[37] and his own delight in language argues for a careful formalist criticism. As with Dashiell Hammett, his self-conscious style provides a meta-fictional commentary on a popular genre, whose aesthetic they both shaped and questioned. But this does not remove their work from history or from the corresponding concerns of writers and artists in less sharply defined areas than hard-boiled fiction. The private eye, whose style and vision Chandler and Hammett were so influential in creating, has proved a genuine popular hero – which is why we need both a formal consciousness and a historical imagination to read popular fictions. For all his anxieties over the demands of a popular form, Chandler believed that such an accommodation was possible: 'My theory has always been that the public will accept style, provided you do not call it style either in words or by, as it were, standing off and admiring it.'[38]

Standing back in self-admiration can be dangerous for the detective as well as the writer. The proof is back in Baltimore, where the detective with a camera eye finally finds and arrests the singer Velma Valento, whom Moose Malloy and Marlowe have been searching for. Velma tries to make a deal but the detective refuses.

> 'Let's go then', she said and stood up and got her coat from a hanger. She went over to him holding the coat out so he could help her into it. He stood up and held it for her like a gentleman. She turned and slipped a gun out of her bag and shot him three times through the coat he was holding.[39]

As Marlowe says, 'the dick had a good eye but he had over specialized'.[40]

Notes

1. Raymond Chandler, *Farewell, My Lovely* (1940) ch. 41; Penguin edn (Harmondsworth, 1949) p. 250.
2. Foreword to Edward Upward's 'The Railway Accident' in *New Directions in Prose and Poetry*, no. 11 (1949); repr. in Upward, *The Railway Accident and Other Stories* (Harmondsworth: Penguin, 1972).
3. Christopher Isherwood, *Goodbye to Berlin* (1939) ch. 1; Triad/Panther edn (London, 1977) p. 11.
4. Wallace Stevens, *Letters* (New York: Alfred A. Knopf, 1966) p. 309.
5. Charles Madge and Tom Harrison, *Britain by Mass Observation* (Harmondsworth: Penguin, 1939) p. 19.
6. John Kobler, *Luce: His Time, Life and Fortune* (New York: Doubleday, 1968) p. 105.
7. Beaumont Newhall, *The History of Photography* (New York: Doubleday, 1964) p. 183.
8. William Stott, *Documentary Expression and Thirties America* (New York: Oxford University Press, 1973) p. 122.
9. James Agee and Walker Evans, *Let Us Now Praise Famous Men* (London: Peter Owen, 1965) p. xii.
10. Quoted in Stott, *Documentary Expression*, p. 272.
11. Agee and Evans, *Let Us Now Praise Famous Men*, p. 11.
12. Ibid., p. 50.
13. Ibid., p. 232.
14. Ernest Hemingway, *Death in the Afternoon* (1932) ch. 1; Penguin edn (Harmondsworth, 1966) p. 6.
15. Graham Greene, *A Gun for Sale* (1936) ch. 1; Penguin edn (Harmondsworth, 1963) p. 6.
16. Ibid., p. 8.
17. Ibid., ch. 3; p. 17.
18. Graham Greene, *Brighton Rock* (1943) pt 1, ch. 1; Penguin edn (Harmondsworth, 1943) pp. 15, 8.
19. Ibid., pt 2, ch. 1; p. 43.
20. William Faulkner, *Sanctuary* (1931) ch. 1; Penguin edn (Harmondsworth, 1953) pp. 5–7.
21. Ibid., p. 5.
22. Ibid.
23. Sinda Gregory, *Private Investigations: The Novels of Dashiell Hammett* (Carbondale: Southern Illinois University Press, 1985) p. 19.
24. Ibid.
25. Dashiell Hammett, *Red Harvest* (1929) ch. 10; in *Four Great Novels* (London: Picador, 1982) p. 79.
26. Russell Nye, *The Unembarrassed Muse: The Popular Arts in America* (New York: Dial Press, 1970) p. 255.
27. Hammett, *Red Harvest*, ch. 4; in *Four Great Novels*, p. 32.
28. Hammett, *Red Harvest*, ch. 21; in *Four Great Novels*, p. 147.
29. Dashiell Hammett, *The Maltese Falcon* (1930) ch. 1; in *Four Great Novels*, p. 375.
30. Hammett, *The Maltese Falcon*, ch. 2; in *Four Great Novels*, p. 382.

31. Frank MacShane, *The Life of Raymond Chandler* (London: Jonathan Cape, 1976) p. 51.
32. Ibid., p. 63.
33. Quoted in Jerry Speir, *Raymond Chandler* (New York: Frederick Ungar, 1981) p. 119.
34. Chandler, *Farewell, My Lovely*, p. 7.
35. Dorothy Gardiner and Katherine Sorley Walker (eds), *Raymond Chandler Speaking* (Boston, Mass.: Houghton Mifflin, 1962) p. 54.
36. Raymond Chandler, *The Lady in the Lake* (1944); Octopus edn (London: Heinemann, 1977) p. 316.
37. Quoted by Philip French in 'Media Marlowes', in Miriam Gross (ed.), *The World of Raymond Chandler* (London: Weidenfeld and Nicolson, 1977) p. 72.

Robert Montgomery's decision to reduce the film to the simple equation of private eye and camera eye has a parallel in an earlier English contribution to the documentary detective story. In 1936, Dennis Wheatley and J. G. Links published *Murder Off Miami*, the first of four 'detective dossiers'. As the Author's Note rightly boasted,

We have pleasure in presenting to the public, between these covers, what we believe to be an entirely new departure in Crime Fiction.

Cablegrams, original handwritten documents, photographs, police reports, criminal records, and even actual clues in the form of human hair, a piece of blood-stained curtain etc., are all contained in this folder, each in its correct order as received at police headquarters, thereby forming the complete Dossier of a crime.

The mystery is presented to the public in exactly the same sequence as that in which it was unravelled by the investigating officer, without any extraneous or misleading matter; photographs of living people taking the place of the descriptions of characters which appear in an ordinary detective novel. Clues to the identity of the murderer are scattered liberally through the investigating officer's reports, and are also to be found in the photographs.

On reaching the end of the investigating officer's fifth report all the available evidence is to hand, yet he finds himself unable to solve the mystery. He then receives instructions to arrest the murderer from his superior, *who has never seen any of the people concerned, but reaches the correct solution of the mystery solely upon the evidence in Dossier form, exactly as it is presented to you here.*

The murderer's confession as to how the crime was committed follows, and the clues which enabled the officer at headquarters to fasten the crime upon him.

Lieutenant John Milton Schwab of the Florida Police Department, who solves the mystery, never appears in the book: he is, to use James Agee's terms, a 'disembodied consciousness', a 'bodyless

eye'. There is no real call on the human imagination when the
murderer can be spotted by his clumsily disguised handwriting and
by the fact that, in assuming his victim's identity and clothing,
Bolitho Blane, the big man of the British soap combine, has not
noticed that the sleeves of the jacket are too short.

38.   Gardiner and Walker, *Raymond Chandler Speaking*, p. 61.
39.   Chandler, *Farewell, My Lovely*, ch. 41; p. 251.
40.   Ibid., p. 250.

4

Investigating the Investigator: Hammett's Continental Op

GARY DAY

If they agree about nothing else, historians of the detective story at least concur in the view that Hammett was a realist. Unlike the writers of the American 'golden age', whose 'main emphasis was on plot ... ingenuity, surprise [and] suspense',[1] he wrote about prohibition, gangsterism and corruption. The argument continues that his detectives, particularly the Continental Op and Sam Spade, were not remote, omniscient figures but involved, fallible ones, who eschewed the literary language of their predecessors and who had more faith in their gun than in the supreme power of reason.

Critics who talk of Hammett's 'objective realism'[2] support their case by referring to his remarks on the contemporary novelist, whose 'job is to take pieces of life and arrange them on paper. . . . The novelist must know how things happen . . . and he must write them down that way.'[3] There is a contradiction here, between the novelist arranging things on paper, and writing them down as he sees them. If he arranges them he is not writing them down as he sees them, and if he writes them down as he sees them then he is not arranging them. This inconsistency complicates the apparently simple idea of realism, making it a less effective way of distinguishing between Hammett's work and that produced in the golden age. If his realism is the product of construction, then it is just as artificial as the elaborately constructed plots of that earlier period.

It is possible to see in the collapse of realism as a distinguishing term the very problem that besets accounts of the detective story[4] – namely, the problem of definition. Historians of the genre variously label it as 'thriller', 'detective story' or 'crime novel',[5] and this

39

failure to agree on definition is significant, for it reproduces the failure within the detective story itself to define who is really the criminal, who is really the detective and what is really the crime. In other words, the problem of identity within the detective story appears in criticism as the problem of how to identify the detective story. The situation is all the more ironic when it is considered that, generally speaking, the detective story promotes the idea that things can be known – a crime is committed and the detective, through deduction or action or both, finds out who is responsible. In many ways the critic is like the detective; he too is faced with clues which he has to fit together in order to produce a true picture of events. Both critic and detective are united in their search for meaning, for the truth hidden behind appearances, but the discovery which neither of them seems to make is that each is like the other. The drama of criticism is played out in the detective story and the drama of the detective story is played out in criticism. There is only the circularity of the text, the reference of one text to another, not to a truth beyond it. In investigating Hammett's Continental Op stories, therefore, there is every chance that this essay will reproduce the very difficulties that the Op himself encounters in the course of his investigations, just as earlier criticism reproduced the difficulties of definition mentioned above.

To say that the Continental Op stories are concerned with knowing is to ask two questions: first, what is known, and, second, how is it known? The first is answered fairly simply – what the Op wants to know of any given situation is 'who' and 'what': 'I hadn't intended putting the slug to him – not until I knew who and what he was' ('The Whosis Kid', p. 172[6]). The terms 'who' and 'what' imply that beneath the confusion of a typical case there is a stable world of persons and things, presences which can be recovered. Indeed, the general pattern of the stories is one of loss and recovery: 'he had employed me to ... find [his] murderers and recover the stolen twenty thousand dollars' ('The Main Death', p. 200). This pattern has its roots in the *fort/da* game where the child, with a toy as a substitute for its mother, alternatively picks it up and throws it down in an attempt to master her presence and her absence, over which he has no real control.[7] Freud sees this as an early attempt at symbolisation, whose characteristic process is to make one thing stand in for another. The result, as in the *fort/da* game, is that the thing recovered is never the thing that was lost. Each repetition, designed to recover the lost object, only succeeds in pushing it further out of reach. The *fort/da* is an elementary form of narrative and shows that there can be no 'real identities' in narrative, only substitutes which vaguely recall them. Thus the 'whos' and 'whats' that the Op sets out to recover are just as misleading as any of the red herrings he may follow up: both lead nowhere, condemning him to repeat the same pattern with the same lack of success in another case.

The Op stories are concerned with 'knowing', which is to be established through a pattern of loss and recovery. However, all this pattern shows is that nothing can be known. In these and other detective stories, a narrative committed to knowing inevitably obscures the object of knowledge. On this basis even the criminal is a substitute, a signifier pointing to a signified which becomes another signifier; in the detective story there are no real solutions, only clues.

The world of 'whos' and 'whats' is not immediately accessible. The Op has to penetrate a number of appearances in order to arrive at it. This aggressive movement is strongly conveyed in the punchy prose style: 'The room was the inside of a black drum on which a giant was beating the long roll. Four guns worked together in a prolonged throbbing roar' ('The Whosis Kid', p. 190). The question of appearances is a difficult one, for they both reflect reality and obscure it. This double character of appearance points to the divided nature of the world in which the Op moves. It is a world that is at once transparent, in the sense that some signifiers are meaningfully bound up with the signifieds, and opaque, in the sense that other signifiers seem to exist independently of any signifieds. 'He was a blond Englishman . . . with all the marks of a gentleman gone to pot on him' ('The Golden Horseshoe', p. 65) is a example of the former, while the 'fragile little old woman, with . . . eyes that twinkled pleasantly behind gold rimmed glasses' ('The House on Turk Street', p. 90) is an example of the latter, as the Op discovers when she betrays him to a gang of crooks.

Both these descriptions are the same in that they focus on externals, yet they are different in the sense that one is 'true' and the other is 'false'. This draws attention to the problematic nature of the sign in the Op's world, and makes it difficult to accept the underlying assumption of the stories, that the outer reality corresponds to the inner one. There can be no correspondence when the actual writing can be shown to be other to itself, as it is in the two quotations. In any case, the distinction between appearance and reality is a false one. Where the signifier relates to the signified the appearance is one with reality, and where it does not the Op invariably discovers the connection that brings them together. In a prose committed to the description of surfaces there is no inner reality. This raises the question of what the Op can know, for to him knowledge is equivalent to the penetration of appearances, but if there are only appearances then there is nothing for him to know. The stories deconstruct themselves by treating appearances as secondary to reality whilst showing that there is no reality except that of appearance. They set out to deny appearances but only demonstrate that they are indispensable. However, criticism needs, like the Op, to forget this if it is to continue its investigation.

The division between the transparent and the opaque in the Op's world is fairly clear cut, but, just as the division between the detective and the criminal occasionally blurs, so the division between these two sometimes disappears, and they merge in the figure of woman. 'The restless black pupils spread out abruptly . . . that was . . . fear . . . But, outside of those . . . pupils, her composure was undisturbed' ('The Tenth Clew', p. 36). The woman's eyes both reveal and conceal her reaction. Her nature is thus the nature of the Op's world, which is both visible and invisible. Moreover, it is woman generally who emerges as the great unknown in these stories. She is the supreme manipulator of appearances and has a disturbing effect on the Op. For example, Elvira, alias Jeanne Delano, 'was a thing to start crazy thoughts even in the head of an unimaginative middle aged thief catcher' ('The Girl with Silver Eyes', p. 142). Woman, in one of the Op's most oft-repeated expressions, 'stirs him up' just as he 'stirs up' crooks. Stirring things up is his system.[8] It is his way of taking control of a situation and finding out about it. When woman stirs him up, however, as Ines does ('she . . . stirred me up inside' – 'The Whosis Kid', p. 170), he is in danger of losing control and also of being known by her.

The Op's relationship to women says something about his relationship to the world, for woman is the world by virtue of the fact that she is both transparent and opaque. Thus, as woman is unknowable, so too is the world and, moreovver, the unknowableness is linked to the way in which she threatens to know the Op. She does this by offering him an image of himself. Ines, like the Op, is 'sure of herself' and her 'work' is 'rough', and it is precisely for this reason, precisely because she is so like him, that the Op is antipathetic to her. His fear of woman is that she is a mirror in which he might see his own face. If woman is like the world and like the Op, then it follows that the Op, in resembling her, also resembles the world. In the end there is no difference between him and the world he investigates, and therefore his particular use of language, for which he claims a superior truth value, loses its transcendent position and becomes equal with those 'lies' he is constantly trying to expose. Knowledge depends on the Ops detached position, but if that position is shown to be false, as it is in the Op's encounter with woman, then knowledge becomes impossible.

How does the Op know what he knows? Occasionally the stories give the impression that events merely confirm what the Op already knows. 'One of two things is going to happen', he says to Kewpie in 'The Golden Horseshoe' (p. 75), and he is proved right. This prescience is supported by the question-and-answer structure of the stories: 'Detectives like questions they already know the answers to' he remarks in *The Dain Curse* (p. 353). There is more concern to endorse existing knowledge than to extend its boundaries, and this points to the conservative character of the stories, for which the question-and-answer structure is responsible. It has its roots in the Socratic dialogue, which in *The Meno* works to produce the claim that 'seeking and learning are in fact nothing but recollection'.[9] However, as Nietzsche has argued, the dialectical method of 'eliciting truth' is 'no more than a rhetorical play', because it forces 'the opponent into a position of weakness *on Socrates' terms*',[10] Rhetoric, rather than rationality, thus seems to lie at the heart of these stories with their stress on finding things out through a process of question and answer. Yet what is found out had to be known at the beginning in order for the story to be written. The narrative logic, which depends on a prior knowledge of the solution, reverses the logic of the detective story, which states that there is first a crime and then a solution.

The reader does not often see the Op working things out; instead, he or she is presented with the Op's conclusions at the end of the story. One example of this is in the last chapter of *The Dain Curse*, where the Op gives a blow-by-blow account of how Owen Fitzstephan was responsible for all the murders in the book. The fact that this explanation is tagged on at the end suggests that how something is known is not satisfactorily integrated with what is known, and also that it is in some sense superflous. For the Op, the superflous account is the false account and must be suppressed. Yet it would seem that his own account of events is also superflous. This indicates another contradiction in these stories: they promote the virtue of economy in explanation and description while at the same time relying on the excesses they condemn.

The Op is continually trying to eliminate the superflous, which he identifies with wordiness. He has a thorough-going contempt for words because they inhibit action ('This jaw-wagging didn't seem to be leading anywhere' – *Red Harvest*, p. 89) and obscure information ('A jumble of words came out of his mouth – "spirited away . . . lured into a trap" – but they were too disconnected for me to make anything out of them' – 'The Girl with Silver Eyes', pp. 110–11). Words are encountered in the form of stories which are appearances that have to be swept away before the Op can reach the truth.

The Op's experience of a situation is through story.[11] At the beginning of 'The Golden Horseshoe' he is given the story of a man called Norman Ashcroft, whilst 'The Girl with the Silver Eyes' commences with the story of Burke Pangburn, who tells of his relationship with Jeanne Delano. Both these stories are shown to be false interpretations of events when the Op investigates them. But stories do not appear only at the beginning of the Op's cases; they run right through them. Each character in a story has a story to tell either about him/herself or events or other characters, and what the Op does in the course of a story is go over all the stories he hears in an attempt to make sense of them. As he puts it, 'You've got to sit down to all the facts you can get and turn them over until they click' (*The Dain Curse*, p. 320). When they do 'click' the result is a clear explanation of events which reveals the connection between one thing and another. As a detective the Op assumes that everything is connected to everything else and it is his job to uncover the connections. Knowledge is knowing how things are connected. However, the Op also suppresses connections. For example, he doesn't want anybody to 'tumble the connection' between himself and Porky in 'The Girl with Silver Eyes' (p. 127), and, furthermore, he himself is detached from everything and everyone around him. In other words, there is a contradiction between the assumption that knowledge depends on discovering connections, the Op's suppression of them, and his separateness from the world he investigates. However, this separateness is untenable, for in his encounter with woman, as I have argued, he is shown to have strong connections with his world. Knowledge depends on connections but the Op suppresses them and seems to assert instead that it depends on his own transcedent position. Once that position is exposed as false, however, the Op is unable to know, even though the interconnectedness of things is at that moment confirmed.

The verb 'to connect' should be contrasted with the verb 'to fit'. As used in the Op stories, 'connect' acquires passive overtones, for connections aren't made – they are discovered. 'Fit' on the other hand is active: 'I spent most of the afternoon putting my findings and guesses on paper and trying to fit them together' (*The Dain Curse*, p. 219). The solution to a case thus becomes a matter of discovery (finding something that was already there) and construction (making of it something that it wasn't originally) and this tension is never quite resolved. As a result it becomes uncertain whether the Op's explanations are true or whether they are merely another story; and the fact that many of the stories end without the Op having sufficient proof for what he believes only increases that doubt.

In investigating other people's stories one of the things that the Op is trying to do is find some connection between the past and present. Until he does, the stories that surround him are deceptive and incomplete. The uncovering of the past thus becomes synonymous with the correcting of story. It also acts as a release: for example, in *Red Harvest* the Op manipulates what he learns of the characters' pasts to purge Poisonville of corruption. The motif of 'digging into [the] past' ('The Tenth Clew', p. 41), as a way of obtaining release and correcting story is familiar from psychoanalysis, and suggests that there may be some similarity between detective stories, the idea behind the talking cure, and the attempt of Freud's patients to get their life stories into some sort of order. Thus the Op stories not only play out the concerns of criticism – they play out those of psychoanalysis too; and this shadowing of texts can hardly be considered surprising when it is remembered that the Op's chief occupation is to discover the relation between different stories.

When the Op looks at another character's story he tends to 'skip ... unnecessary words' (*The Dain Curse*, p. 315), reducing it to its bare essentials. For instance, the rambling account that Murray Abernathy gives of Creda Dexter 'amounted to this' ('The Tenth

Clew', p. 34), and the Op economically recounts what he has just heard. Weeding out excess words is equivalent to obtaining knowledge, for they conceal the truth instead of revealing it. On this formation truth is identified with what is clear, simple and short and this exactly describes the style in which the stories are written.[12] This makes truth indistinguishable from style and emphasises its rhetorical, rather than its factual, nature. Nevertheless, clarity, simplicity and brevity are regarded by the Op as characteristics of truth, and it is with these criteria that he interprets other people's stories, which he finds are fictions, creating false realities or distorting the actual one, mere superfluities which have to be disposed of.

Disposing of them involves either disproving them or eliciting what little truth they may contain. Thus the story that the Op tells the reader is an interpretation of the stories he hears, which in turn are interpretations, albeit false ones, of the characters and events that he is investigating by interpreting the stories that he hears, and so on in a circular fashion. Moreover, by repeating these stories to the reader as a means of recounting his interpretation of them, the Op's own story comes to depend on repetition; yet repetition is a form of superfluity and as such must be condemned.

Many characters the Op encounters repeat themselves. In *The Dain Curse* the Op quickly silences the night clerk because he doesn't want 'to hear the story all over again' (p. 283), while in *Red Harvest* he prevents Bob McSwain from repeating himself by interrupting the 'merry-go-round' (p. 68). This suppression of repetition, however, is not extended to his own stories, each of which follows the same basic pattern: that is, a crime occurs which he solves. The repetition of this structure in each new story suggests that repetition has a positive, as well as a negative, character. This is illustrated in *The Dain Curse*. There the Op is trying to persuade Gabrielle Dain that the things that have happened to her are not the result of some supernatural agency but can be rationally explained: ' "Can you remember what you told me last night?" she asked. . . . "Yeah." "Tell me again", she begged. "Sit down and tell me again – all of it." I did' (p. 336).

Here repetition is intended to reassure. Specifically it is meant to assert the superiority of one discourse over another – namely, the irrational story of the curse. Throughout, the Op is concerned to promote the rational over the story, but the rational is just as much a matter of style and repetition as is story, and so it remains inextricably tied to that from which it tries to differentiate itself.

The Op does not prove that the rational discourse is the truthful one; he merely repeats his claim that it is. Lack of proof is a recurrent motif in the Op stories and once more raises the question of what can be known. Many of his cases end with his being unable to prove the guilt of the person whom he believes is guilty. 'I couldn't prove it' he says in 'The Farewell Murder' (p. 253), whilst in 'The Main Death' the wife says her husband has 'no definite proof' against her (p. 218). However, this lack of proof in the stories is not to be understood as the text's consciousness that its claims to truth are without proof; rather it is the text's very unconsciousness of this problem which raises it to a level different from the one where it originated. This dislocation condemns the stories to repetition and may also be responsible for the way one thing is always seen in terms of another. The handkerchief in 'The Main Death', for example, is not just a handkerchief; it is also a clue, a signifier whose real significance lies in its relation to a gun and a wallet. Nothing can be proved because nothing, in these stories, is truly itself; it is always something other.[13]

The Op overcomes this lack of proof by tricking his victims into confessing. At the end of 'The Farewell Murder', for instance, he makes a dead man's head appear to nod in answer to the question of Ringgo's guilt, and the latter, believing that the dead man had really nodded, confesses. What happens, in other words, is that the Op resorts to fiction to prove a character's guilt. Thus, although he is constantly trying to root out fiction, he depends on it to do the very job that it is not supposed to be able to do: to prove that such and such was the case.

The lack of proof which plagues the Op brings about a split between knowledge and belief: 'I don't know . . . I'd rather believe I saw things that weren't there' (*The Dain Curse*, p. 279). The Op believes that something is true even though he can't prove it, and therefore doesn't know that it is. This type of thinking – believing without knowing – is exactly the sort of thinking of which he tries to rid Gabrielle Dain. The irony is not only that he himself thinks that way but that it is the inadequacy of his rational vision which makes him do so. In setting out to prove the superiority of the rational he only succeeds in showing the need for its opposite. He affirms what he originally denied.

The distinction between the Op's rational account or explanation of events and the story is further undermined by the contradictory way in which he tries to expose the latter. In order to discover the truth he frequently resorts to lying: 'I concocted a wonderful series of lies ... that I thought would get me the information I wanted' ('The Main Death', p. 209). He uses fiction to penetrate fiction. Further, the words 'game' and 'play' consistently describe both his and his opponents' orchestrations of events. He uses the elements of story, game, play and fabrication to disprove 'story', but by that action 'proves' both its necessity and its indispensability as a way of making sense of experience. Indeed, in a world where nothing is known the only possible way of organising experience is through story. And this is exactly what the Op does when he 'writes up' his cases. His trick, however, is to conflate the logic of the story – with its beginning, middle and end – with the logic of 'truth', so that his story appears as truth whilst everyone else's simply appears as fiction.

As story the Op's discourse can claim no special privileges of explanation. In fact, as story it does not explain events, but merely retells them. According to the Op, a rational discourse alone has the power of explanation, but, as there is only the illusion of rational discourse in these stories, there are no explanations, just retellings. For example, the final chapter of *The Dain Curse* simply retells, in summary form, the whole story from Fitzstephan's point of view, and a similar case can be made for most of the short stories.

It should not be thought, however, that the logic of story is any clearer than the logic of explanation; it is just as confused and contradictory, not the least because it refuses to tell a tale. The story that the Op tells conceals within it another story, that of the Op.

Although the Op wants to rid his world of words that conceal the truth, he also uses them for that purpose. In *Red Harvest* he doesn't 'report all the distressing details' (p. 107) of his activities in Poisonville. The word 'detail' is interesting because it points to another contradictory meaning in these stories. In the first place, it is a form of superfluity and must therefore be repressed, but, in the second place, the Op, as detective, depends on detail in order to solve his cases. 'Detailed work occupied all of us', he says in 'The Golden Horseshoe' (p. 71). The reason the Op suppresses the details of his activities in Poisonville is because they show that he behaved little better than the crooks he was hired to remove from the town. His feelings of guilt, however, are not confined to this story but recur in others.

In 'The Farewell Murder', for instance, he fails to save the man he was supposed to protect, and the rest of the story becomes a defence of his 'skill as a sleuth' (p. 252). A vague sense of guilt pervades most of the stories. The word 'admit', which is frequently used, even on the most innocuous occasions, is one sign of this. Characters admit who they are, as if there was something criminal about their identity: ' "You're another detective aren't you?" I admitted that' (*The Dain Curse*, p. 195). Talking too much is another sign of guilt: 'You talked too much son. That's a way you amateur criminals have. You've always got to overdo the frank and open business' (*Red Harvest*, p. 56). In contrast, the Op is closed and secret, writing in a bare style shorn of detail, its muteness an assertion of innocence.

The Op admits his guilt in the context of a specific situation, but denies it through the very style in which the stories are written. Even when he admits it, however, it is only to blame other characters or events beyond his control. Thus in *Red Harvest* he puts the blame for his behaviour on Poisonville ('It's what this place has done to me' – p. 142), and Dinah Brand ('You seem to have a gift for stirring up murderous notions in your boyfriends. Even I haven't escaped your influence' – p. 143).

This projection of guilt ties in with a recurrent theme of the stories – that of the 'frame-up'. It is particularly prominent in *The Dain Curse*, and there it is specifically linked with literature, for the main character is a writer who skilfully ensures that he is never made accountable for his actions. This suggests that writing a story is like planning a frame-up. Moreover, in order to be successful, the frame-up has to have a tight structure that makes it plausible and convincing. Perhaps it can be suggested that the tight structure of the detective story is not a demonstration of an all-inclusive rationality, but a way of unloading irrational impulses onto another so that the detective can then appear penetrating and logical. If this is the case, then the first principle of the detective story is not 'reason' but the creation of appearances – the very thing it sets out to expose.

The story that the Op has to tell never gets told, because of the stories he tells about other characters. It is difficult to know whether he tells these stories because they demonstrate his method or because they hide his own story. Certainly, many of his cases, with their detailed account of his thoughts and movements, read as if he were the accused being cross-examined in the witness box. What he would be doing there in the first place, however, is another matter. His identification with criminals and vague suggestions of guilt operate as clues but ones which do not seem to fit together.

Perhaps this may have something to do with the way in which not only these, but also other, detective stories are a mixture of repressed, conflicting narratives. The Op's guilt suggests a confessional narrative, while the motif of search can be traced back to the Holy Grail. The Gothic irruption of evil into an otherwise ordered world is another narrative strand, not to mention the many ballads and pamphlets dealing with criminals and crime. In addition to these, and by no means the last on the list, are the investigations of social science, which in their concentration on detail also contribute something to the development of the detective story. Approaching it from this angle, it is more a relation of texts to one another than a single text with a claim to truth.[14]

If the detective story is undermined as a discourse of knowing because of the cacophony of texts within it, then what remains? It has been interpreted in terms of the Oedipal myth and the primal scene[15] but this is merely to reproduce the detective's own activity. He too takes the clues and makes of them something 'other', but the workings of the texts show this to be a false procedure. The detective's search for causes, which he identifies with meaning, are themselves effects. The Op penetrates stories to reach the truth behind them, but in the process it is revealed that truth is a function of the style of his own story – clear, simple and short. Story, which was to be dispensed with as something secondary, turns out to be primary and indispensable. This reversal collapses the claim of the rational discourse of sole access to truth. Furthermore, if cause is itself an effect, then not only the claims of rational discourse disappear but so does the discourse itself, which was based on the logic of cause and effect. 'If either cause or effect can occupy the position of origin, then origin is no longer originary.'[16] It is no longer who is guilty of the crime, or what is the crime that causes the guilt, for it is impossible to decide on a prior cause.

To a certain extent the Op recognises this paradoxical state of affairs. For example, he sometimes refers to the solution of a case as a 'story'. 'There isn't much story', he says in 'The Main Death'

(p. 217), as he begins an account of what he has learnt. Here story has taken over the function of explanation. It can do this because the narrative logic of the story, with its beginning, middle and end, corresponds to the logic of explanation which tries to show that there is an ordered sequence of events. However, because the two are so closely intertwined, it is inevitable that, once the logic of the one collapses, that of the other will too. Thus story, which was at first seen as concealing truth, replaces explanation as a way of revealing it, but in that very revelation conceals the story of the Op and so comes full circle. Is there any way of escaping from this circularity?

One aspect of these stories which may repay investigation concerns the way in which the Op asserts himself. The reader is never in any doubt that the Op knows more than the other characters and is stronger than they are: 'It was time for me to do something. I had let these comedians run the show for long enough' ('The Whosis Kid', p. 187). The purpose of such remarks, and there are many of them, is to show that the Op is a particular type of man, tough, cool and in absolute control, and it is in this capacity that he tries to win the reader's approval and recognition. If these stories are seen as attempts by the Op to win recognition, then his laconic manner and grim humour show that the discourse which prioritises knowledge must also persuade the reader of the integrity of the knower. However, a sleight of hand is at work here, for the reader is not persuaded of the Op's ability to know by the way he solves the problems, but by the rhetorical devices mentioned above which have nothing to do with knowing as such. Furthermore, the Op offers himself as the guarantee of knowledge of his world, on the basis of his self-knowledge: "Knowing myself, I'm sure of it", I insisted' ('The Main Death', p. 211). However, he keeps the knowledge of himself from the reader, who only knows that the Op is not unlike his adversaries and that, as in *Red Harvest*, he is easily influenced by his surroundings. All that is left, then, is for his to 'insist' on the reader's recognition and in this he is replaying with the reader his relations with other characters.

As another character, the reader may occupy the position of 'the Old Man', the chief of the Agency for whom the Op works, and whom the Op fears and respects, and to whom he sends his reports for reading. The Old Man thus functions as a fixed point in the text. In that capacity he is the Father, the Other, the source of meaning. The problem is that this is precisely the position that the

Op tries to occupy and so the Old Man or the reader becomes his rival. In struggling to occupy the position from which he seeks recognition, the Op once more shows himself to be a contradictory figure.

However, to pursue the role of the reader in these stories, to show how the Op addresses him or her in a manner similar to the way in which he addresses other characters, or to show in more detail how the reader is inserted into the position of the Old Man and why, would only be to follow more clues, which would lead to other clues, and so on in an endless series. So, like the Op, the reader must decide on an interpretation if he or she is to close the signifying chain. The problem is that the scene of interpretation is scattered with clues which point to its arbitrary nature, thereby undermining its claim to truth. This is the trajectory of the Continental Op stories. They implicitly assert that what is hidden can be revealed, but the act of revelation involves hiding the false logic on which that revelation depends. The text thus doubles itself in a contradictory movement. The Op explains by disproving story, yet his explanations are themselves stories which conceal another story. Consequently, to know is not to uncover the repressed – it *is* to repress; and, with this paradoxical reversal of meaning, meaning itself collapses. The Op arrives at the place he first started from because he has only succeeded in duplicating the very condition he was trying to remove.

Looking at the way the Op solicits recognition may offer one escape from this circularity, until it is realised that the Op's demand is based on self-knowledge – the area in which he is most blind. A shift to reader-oriented criticism would fare no better, since that would inevitably lead to the recognition that the reader only reproduces the texts he or she investigates, which, like the Op, means that he or she knows by not knowing. To say more would merely be to prolong that repetition.

Notes

1. Ellery Queen, quoted in Mike Pavett, 'From the Golden Age to Mean Streets', in H. R. F. Keating (ed.), *Crime Writers* (London: BBC, 1978) p. 78.
2. W. F. Nolan, *Dashiell Hammett: A Casebook* (Santa Barbara, Calif.: McNally and Loftin, 1969) p. 3.
3. Hammett, quoted ibid., p. 5.

4. I shall use the phrase 'detective story' throughout this chapter. It is to be understood as a label of convenience.

5. See, for example, Julian Symons, *Bloody Murder* (Harmondsworth: Penguin, 1975); Jerry Palmer, *Thrillers: Genesis and Structure of a Popular Genre* (London: Edward Arnold, 1978); and Howard Haycraft, *Murder for Pleasure* (New York and London: Appleton-Century, 1941).

6. All quotations from the short stories are from Dashiell Hammett, *The Continental Op*, selected and with an introduction by Steven Marcus (London: Picador, 1984). Quotations from the novels are from Hammett, *The Four Great Novels: 'The Dain Curse'; 'The Glass Key'; 'The Maltese Falcon'; and 'Red Harvest'* (London: Picador, 1982). Page references are given in the text.

7. Sigmund Freud, 'Beyond the Pleasure Principle', in *Standard Edition of the Complete Works of Sigmund Freud*, ed. James Strachey, xviii (London: Hogarth Press, 1974) pp. 9–64, esp. pp. 15–17.

8. See Steven Marcus's introductory essay to *The Continental Op*, p. 17.

9. Plato, *Protagorus and Meno*, tr. W. K. C. Guthrie (Harmondsworth: Penguin, 1972) p. 130.

10. Christopher Norris, *Deconstruction: Theory and Practice* (London: Methuen, 1982) p. 60.

11. See Marcus, introductory essay to *The Continental Op*.

12. This style could also be described as staccato, one thing following another without connection, yet connection is one of the prime features of the detective story. This is an area which would repay further investigation.

13. In this the detective story resembles myth, where one thing is explained in terms of another. There are other similarities between the 'structure' of myth and the 'structure' of the detective story, such as ahistorical vision and a total world view in which there is no conception of difference, but there is not space to go into that here.

14. Jerry Palmer, 'The Literary Origins of The Thriller', in *Thrillers*.

15. Symons, *Bloody Murder*, pp. 12–13.

16. J. Culler, *On Deconstruction: Theory and Criticism after Structuralism* (Routledge and Kegan Paul, 1983) p. 88.

5

Radical Anger: Dashiell Hammett's *Red Harvest*

CHRISTOPHER BENTLEY

I

Dashiell Hammett's life, in its discontinuities and contradictions, seems to embody the uneasy pluralism of American society.[1] Born into a Southern Catholic family, he worked for some years as an investigator for the Pinkerton Detective Agency, which often functioned as the private police of America's mineowners.[2] Both world wars found him willing to defend America, but in the 1950s he appeared in court, and before Senator McCarthy's Senate Internal Security Subcommittee, as a known Communist sympathiser. The fiction on which his reputation rests was written within the space of twelve years. Hammett wrote no definitive account of his political and social beliefs. The challenge to his radicalism, the need to define and to defend, came quite late in life, and after the age of thirty-nine Hammett found it difficult to write anything. The opinions of these later years survive mainly in remarks recalled by Hammett's long-standing friend and protector, Lillian Hellman, such as his assertion the night before he went to jail for refusing to reveal the names of contributors to the bail-bond fund of the Civil Rights Congress, 'I hate this damn kind of talk, but maybe I better tell you that if it were more than jail, if it were my life, I would give it for what I think democracy is and I don't let cops or judges tell me what I think democracy is.'[3]

By this time Hammett was willing to suffer for his beliefs, but unable to write about them. (Ironically, though a novelist of violence, Hammett was always more of a victim than a fighter: serving in the Motor Ambulance Corps in the First World War, he was assigned to a camp twenty miles from his home in Baltimore and developed tuberculosis; in the Second World War he edited an army newspaper in the Aleutians and contracted emphysema;

after that war his allegiance to Communism brought him six months in a federal prison and further damage to his health.) In later life Hammett was capable only of the martyr's gesture (apparently he did not know the names he was jailed for refusing to reveal), but while still a writer he had allowed some of his fiction to express his hostility to American capitalism. Though he probably did not become a Communist until 1937 or 1938, it is in his earliest writing that his radicalism is most evident.

Hammett's first successful detective (after a couple of false starts) is the Continental Op, perhaps less well known than Sam Spade or Nick Charles because less exploited by the cinema. The Op – named only by his occupation – appears in thirty-six short stories, published chiefly in *Black Mask* between October 1923 and November 1930, and in two novels, *Red Harvest* and *The Dain Curse*, both revisions of four-part story sequences in *Black Mask*, and both published in 1929. All Continental Op narratives are told in the first person. The Op is aged between thirty-five and forty, short and overweight, but able to give a good account of himself in a fight. He carries a .38 Special revolver and often uses it. Little of his private life or history appears in the stories, but he held a captain's commission in wartime military intelligence, and speaks French and bad German.[4] He is single, and lives in an apartment in San Francisco. Many of his cases take place in that city, which he knows intimately, though his investigations are likely to send him anywhere in America, and even to Mexico and to Europe.[5]

Unlike such successors as Sam Spade, Philip Marlowe and Lew Archer, he is not a self-employed investigator, waiting in his office for clients, but an employee of the Continental Detective Agency. His cases begin when the Old Man, head of the Agency's San Franciso office, calls him in and hands him a job. Thus the Op is accountable not only to the law (though his relations with the San Francisco police are surprisingly good) but also to his employers, who require reports at the conclusion of a case. However, unlike the self-employed detective, he can call on the resources of a large organisation. The Agency is reputable – it handles no divorce work – and has 'rather strict' rules for its employees, forbidding them, for example, to accept reward money. The Op, an ideal organisation man, works only for 'a fair salary' and for love of the job: 'I like being a detective, like the work. And liking work makes you want to do it as well as you can. . . . I can't imagine a pleasanter future than twenty-some years more of it.'[6] However, when the Op's gratitude to the employers who are making this future possible extends to arranging the killing of a corrupt fellow operative to protect the good name of the Agency, one sees that he has something in common with Norman Mailer's hoodlum policemen who 'will put up with poor salary' because 'they know they are lucky; they know they are getting away with a successful solution to the criminality they can taste in their blood'.[7] The Op is frequently, and sometimes gratuitously, violent, and enjoys the violence as much as any other part of his work:

> It was a swell bag of nails. Swing right, swing left, kick, swing right, swing left, kick. Don't hesitate, don't look for targets. God will see that there's always a mug there for your gun or blackjack to sock, a belly for your foot.

And on another occasion:

> I got my left arm around his body, holding him where I wanted him. And I began to throw my right fist into him.
> I liked that. His belly was flabby, and it got softer every time I hit it. I hit it often.[8]

His loyalty to his employers and to his work has no moral dimension, and is merely pride in a job that gives meaning to his life, providing acceptable outlets for his violence and need for power. Garry Wills speaks of Hammett's detectives as 'serving society without respecting it'.[9] The Op is not a man to say much about society, but certainly he shows little respect or liking for many of the Agency's clients, who almost inevitably have money, and some of whom are very wealthy.

The first *Black Mask* story to carry Hammett's name, and one of the earliest Continental Op stories, 'Crooked Souls' (Oct 1923; retitled 'The Gatewood Caper' in Hammett collections), introduces a client, Harvey Gatewood, who 'had made his several millions by sandbagging everybody that stood in his way' and 'with his war contracts still being investigated by the Department of Justice'. His nineteen-year-old daughter Audrey, is kidnapped, and he receives a ransom note which concludes, '$50,000 is only a small fraction of what you stole while we were living in mud and blood in France for you, and we mean to get that much or else!' The Op admits, 'I didn't like him either personally or by reputation', but he tackles the case with his usual skill, and establishes that the daughter, a drug-user and hell-raiser, had arranged her own kidnapping to extract money from her father. They are reunited at police headquarters: 'it was a merry little party', says the Op, savouring the troubles of the rich. Audrey intimidates her father with 'a threat of spilling everything she knew about him to the newspapers'; the police do not bring charges; and father and daughter leave for home together, 'sweating hate for each other from every pore'.[10]

A later writer might have been tempted to present this conflict of generations in political or social terms, the daughter having developed a conscience about her father's wartime profiteering; Hammett sees it as Audrey's desperate bid for independence: 'If *you'd* been tied to him as long as I have and had been bullied and held down as much, I guess *you'd* do most anything to get enough money so that you could go away and live your own life.'[11] Apart from the accusation in the ransom note (which purports to come from an embittered war veteran), there is no social retribution in her actions: in the Op's cliché, she is 'a chip off the old block', and, like her father, wants money at any price. The Op recognises their moral resemblance: 'Remembering some of the business methods Harvey Gatewood had used ... I suppose the worst that could be said about Audrey was that she was her father's own daughter.'[12] Both share an innate criminality – Audrey's manifesting itself in a cruder form – and both seem to be getting away with it. Audrey will not be prosecuted for the fake kidnapping, and in return she will not reveal her father's secrets; therefore he will probably never be made to account for his war contracts.

'The Gutting of Couffignal' (*Black Mask*, Dec 1925) finds the Op on a small island in San Pablo Bay, mostly inhabited by

> well-fed old gentlemen who, the profits they took from the world with both hands in their younger days now stowed away at safe percentages, have bought into the island colony so they may spend what is left of their lives nursing their livers and improving their golf among their kind. They admit to the island only as many storekeepers, working people, and similar riffraff as are needed to keep them comfortably served.[13]

The Op has been hired to guard the presents at a society wedding on the island, and, though courteously treated by his clients and the wedding guests, is clearly one of the 'working people, and similar riffraff'. Couffignal's inhabitants, 'in their younger days' the aggressors, now become the victims. A gang of exiled White Russian aristocrats and generals destroy the bridge linking Couffignal to the mainland and, using explosives, machine guns, and small arms, proceed to gut the island, systematically looting the bank, the stores, and the houses of the wealthy. But the Russians are themselves victims of Bolshevism. Though they have been passing as wealthy residents of Couffignal, they are in fact almost penniless, having spent the capital they brought with them from Russia. They have tried, and failed in, honest ways of making a living in exile, and this crime is a despairing attempt to get enough money to retain what they see as their rightful place in society. Their spokeswoman defiantly justifies this wholesale robbery to the Op: 'Could it be said that we owed the world and fealty? Had not the world sat idly by and seen us despoiled of place and property and country?'[14] However, as in Audrey Gatewood's caper, there is little social criticism implied in their actions: they want to rejoin the exploiting class, not to abolish it. Hammett describes the gutting of this wealthy island with undisguised pleasure, but the process is easily reversible. The Op discovers the guilty, they will be arrested, and the plunder will be restored. As in the earlier story, the wealthy are saved. The only people killed in Couffignal's night are violence of the police chief, a chauffeur, and a butler – all 'working people'. The Op is allowed to dislike the rich, but Hammett protects them.

II

The fullest fictional expression of Hammett's radicalism – and its limits – is found in his earliest novel, *Red Harvest* (1929; first published as four stories in *Black Mask*, Nov 1927 – Feb 1928). The plot is complex and defies brief summary, but its premises may be readily stated. The Op arrives in Personville, a blighted industrial city usually called 'Poisonville', in response to a letter sent to the Continental Detective Agency's San Francisco branch by newspaper publisher Donald Willsson asking that an operative come to Personville 'to do some work for him'. Willsson is murdered before the Op meets him, and, in conversation with a labour organiser, Bill Quint, the Op discovers that

For forty years old Elihu Willsson – father of the man who had been killed this night – had owned Personville, heart, soul, skin and guts. He was president and majority stockholder of the Personville Mining Corporation, ditto of the First National Bank, owner of the *Morning Herald* and *Evening Herald*, the city's only newspapers, and at least part owner of nearly every other enterprise of any importance. Along with these pieces of property he owned a United States senator, a couple of representatives, the governor, the mayor, and most of the state legislature. Elihu Willsson was Personville, and he was almost the whole state. (pp. 8–9[15])

During the war the Industrial Workers of the World had unionised the city; but in 1921, taking advantage of a business recession, Elihu Willsson had repudiated his agreements with his employees, and 'began kicking them back into their pre-war circumstances'. Bill Quint, representing the IWW (or 'wobblies'), advised industrial sabotage, but the workers preferred a strike, which lasted eight months. 'Both sides bled plenty. The wobblies had to do their own bleeding. Old Elihu hired gunmen, strike-breakers, national guardsmen and even parts of the regular army, to do his. When the last skull had been cracked, the last rib kicked in, organized labor in Personville was a used firecracker' (p. 9). But Elihu then found himself unable to get rid of the gunmen he had imported: 'They had won his strike for him and they took the city for their spoils. He couldn't openly break with them. They had too much on him. He was responsible for all they had done during the strike' (p. 10). Personville is presently divided between Pete the Finn, whose gang supplies the bootleg liquor; Lew Yard, who 'does a lot of bail bond business' and handles stolen goods; and Max 'Whisper' Thaler, who runs the gambling. Noonan, the chief of police, is as corrupt as the gangsters, and his force is essentially a fourth gang. Bill Quint believes that Elihu was using Donald, who edited the newspapers for his father, in a devious attempt to rid himself of the gangsters by 'a reform campaign in the papers', and that some of the gangsters had killed him: 'The old man's using the boy to shake 'em loose. I guess they got tired of being shook' (p. 10).

This is the situation confronting the Op. The Agency's client is already dead, so, strictly speaking, the Op's assignment has ended. But he remains in Personville to hunt for Donald Willsson's killer. Elihu wants to believe that his son's wife ('that French hussy') killed him, but the Op ominously insists that 'the other angle has got to be looked into too – the political end' (p. 16). He discovers that Donald Willsson was killed by a young bank cashier named Albury, rejected lover of one Dinah Brand, 'a de luxe hustler, a big-league gold-digger', in the mistaken belief that the wealthy newspaper editor was buying Dinah's favours. It was a private murder, motivated by jealousy, and only incidentally connected with 'Personville politics' through Dinah Brand's association with the gangsters, some of whose secrets she had sold to Donald Willsson to be used in his reform campaign. In the meantime, Elihu Willsson has been frightened and angered by an attempt on his life, and hires the Op to clean up the town. This is the opportunity he has been waiting for. He demands 'a free hand – no favors to anybody – run the job as I pleased', and promises – or threatens – Elihu that he is 'going to get a complete job or nothing' (pp. 40–1). At the Op's insistence, a cheque and a letter confirming his assignment are sent to the Continental Detective Agency; but from now on the Op behaves more like a vigilante than a private detective. As he tells two colleagues from the Agency who join him later, 'there's no use taking anybody into court, no matter what you've got on them. They own the courts, and, besides, the courts are too slow for us now' (p. 110). The Op's clean-up is complicated and bloody. He contrives mutual suspicion among the gangsters, playing off one faction against another.[16] By the end of the novel most of the important characters have died violently, gang warfare has contributed many more minor victims, and Personville is under martial law.

Whatever detective work the Op does is of a casual nature, as he is more concerned to create trouble than to clear it up. *Red Harvest* offers few of the satisfactions of the classical detective story with its developmental structure comprising a series of discoveries leading to a concluding revelation. Certain murders are solved, almost incidentally, in a discrete sequence; but the novel focuses on the Op's clean-up and the nature of the community that is to be purged.

At the same time, *Red Harvest* attempts to divert sympathy from Personville by insisting on the polluted ugliness of the city (even its summer resort, suspiciously named Mock Lake, is a 'dump') and on the squalid lives of its inhabitants. Personville is utterly inimical to physical beauty and moral integrity. Dinah Brand, 'who took her pick of Poisonville's men', has 'the face of a girl of twenty-five already showing signs of wear ... large eyes, blue and a bit bloodshot', and a perpetual run in her stocking (p. 30). She lives with a consumptive in a sordid, cluttered, frame cottage, and betrays her friends eagerly for money, selling one of them to the Op in a grotesque auction which earns her $200.10. Unwittingly emphasising her own coarseness, she reminisces about an acquaintance 'back in England now' who 'used to wear white silk socks turned inside out so the loose threads wouldn't hurt his feet' (p. 81). Obviously such an exquisite could not stand Personville for long. The poisoning effect of this environment is embodied in Myrtle Jennison, who two years before had been 'a classy looking kid ... a slender blonde'; now she is 'dying of Bright's disease or something'. As she has information about a murder, the Op visits her in hospital: 'Her face was a bloated spotty mask ... with ugly eyes that were shaded into no particular dark color by the pads of flesh around them ... a horrible swollen body in a coarse white nightgown' (pp. 81, 86). Other sick or damaged people appear, but like Myrtle they evoke revulsion rather than sympathy. The gangster Max Thaler has 'something wrong with his throat' and speaks in a 'hoarse whispering voice'. Even thin, tubercular Dan Rolff, with his educated voice (curiously like Hammett), though obviously a cut above his environment, is treated with the same objective harshness. The city itself is sometimes presented as a human body, but a body to be butchered: Elihu Willsson owns it, 'heart, soul, skin and guts', and the Op promises to open it up 'from Adam's apple to ankles'. The novel indulges its punishing narrator, not the suffering community.

Our view of Personville's inhabitants is also insidiously prejudiced by images of animality. Many of these are common comparisons, but their cumulative effect is striking. Donald Willsson's father 'used him for his monkey'; Helen Albury is 'crazy as a bedbug'; Personville is a 'pig-sty' and Elihu wants the Op to 'smoke out the rats'; policemen are 'bulls'; Reno Starkey has a 'sallow horse face' and is 'Yard's pup'; he and the other gangsters are 'wolves'; the Op is 'a damned little woolly lamb' playing the gangsters 'like you'd play trout'. The animal virtually obliterates the humanity of one character, Bob MacSwain, an ex-policeman and 'small-time grifter'. He has 'a long sharp jaw, like a hog's', a comparison reiterated so insistently at almost every mention of him that his name begins to echo 'swine'. No wonder that the Op finally gets him where a hog should be, 'down on his knees in the muddy alley'. MacSwain was warned: at their first meeting the Op had introduced himself, not entirely untruthfully, with 'a name, something like Hunter' (pp. 66, 105).

Throughout his red harvest, the Op's motives remain fundamentally unclear. The murder of the Agency's first client, Donald Willsson, does not spur him to vindicate his professional competence and the Agency's reputation. Personville affronts him aesthetically ('an ugly city of forty thousand people, set in an ugly notch between two ugly mountains that had been all dirtied up by mining'); but, even though his description suggests that Personville is the arsehole of America, this seems an inadequate reason for the destructive intelligence and energy he directs at the community. Nor is his crusade inspired by respect for the law: as a regular drinker of bootleg liquor and an occasional user of laudanum, he has fallen a long way from his grand archetype, Allan Pinkerton, who 'had never tasted liquor, had never allowed it in his house, and had never smoked'.[17] There is no one in Personville whom the Op wishes to protect. He makes many acquaintances, but no friends; and acquaintances are to be used or betrayed. Indeed, to know the Op is to run a real risk of death, for he is as much a murderer as his gangland enemies. He shoots a policeman to establish his bona fides with the gangsters, and later cold-bloodedly sends the chief of police to his death.

When Elihu Willsson tries to dispense with his services, the Op does discover a personal motive:

> Your fat chief of police tried to assassinate me last night. I don't like that. I'm just mean enough to want to ruin him for it. Now I'm going to have my fun. I've got ten thousand dollars of your money to play with. I'm going to use it opening Poisonville up from Adam's apple to ankles. (p. 60)

But the indignation is rhetorical and spurious. A detective may reasonably expect the occasional attempt on his life (though perhaps not often by a chief of police). In any case, the Op had already set his trouble-making machinery in motion, and his reaction is grossly in excess of any provocation offered him. As one gangster remarks, 'I hear you've declared war on Poisonville.' It is fallacious to say that 'the Op's mission changes from a professional one to a personal one as he becomes corrupted by the corrupt world in which he finds himself'.[18] He had brought his skill, his ruthlessness, and his violence to town with him, looking for a job. Personville's corruption has its origins in the desire for money and power, and is therefore explicable, even rational. Indifferent to money and to the ostentatious kind of power exercised in Personville (his preference being the covert power that comes from a knowlege of men's secrets and weaknesses), the Op is as incorruptible as Robespierre, and just as deadly to the community, while his motives have the unfathomable irrationality of fanaticism.

The Op's own attempt to blame Personville for his actions is unconvincing. During a drinking session with Dinah Brand, a sympathetic listener, he becomes maudlin and repetitious:

> I put my glass on the table, sat down facing it, and complained:
>   'This damned burg's getting me. If I don't get away soon I'll be going blood-simple like the natives. . . . I've arranged a killing or two in my time, when they were necessary. But this is the first time I've ever got the fever. It's this damned burg. You can't go straight here. I got myself tangled at the beginning. When old Elihu ran out on me there was nothing I could do but try to set the boys against each other. I had to swing the job the best way I could. How could I help it if the best way was bound to lead to a lot of killing? . . . It's this damned town. Poisonville is right. It's poisoned me . . . this getting a rear out of planning deaths is not natural to me. It's what this place has done to me. . . . I'm going blood-simple.' (pp. 142–6)

And so on. It is evident that he is experiencing considerable strain, and understandable that he should try to exculpate himself by placing the responsibility on Personville; but his recapitulation of recent events is inaccurate and his self-justification is mostly bluster.. His credibility is further weakened by an abrupt change of tactics, as he suddenly tries to blame it all on Dinah Brand: 'Forgotten that Donald Willsson was killed because of you, starting the whole thing? Forgotten that it was the dope you gave me on Whisper that kept the job from petering out in the middle?' (p. 147). Though Dinah is not exactly a guiltless woman, this is a sophistical twisting of the facts. When Dinah's gin and laudanum have ceased to work in him, the Op will have only himself to accuse.

It has been suggested that the violence of the Op (and other *Black Mask* heroes) is 'a kind of meaningful violence, sometimes symbolic of a special ethical code or attitude, sometimes an explicit description and implicit criticism of a corrupt society'.[19] Apart from his narrow and sometimes questionable professionalism, it is hard to see that the Op has any ethical code, or that his violence is any more meaningful than that it serves to keep him alive and to kill people whom he wishes to see dead. However, *Red Harvest* does contain much explicit description and implicit criticism of one very corrupt city, and by extension the corruption of capitalist society, observed in the microcosm of Personville. 'And what else is Personville', claims Steven Marcus, 'except Leviathan, the "artificial man" represented by Hobbes as the image of society itself?'

One can thus make out quite early in this native American writer a proto-Marxist critical representation of how a certain kind of society works. Actually, the point of view is pre- rather than proto-Marxist, and the social world as it is dramatized in many of these stories is Hobbesian rather than Marxist. It is a world of universal warfare, the war of each against all, and of all against all. The only thing that prevents the criminal ascendancy from turning into permanent tyranny is that the crooks who take over society cannot cooperate with one another, repeatedly fall out with each other, and return to the Hobbesian anarchy out of which they have momentarily arisen.[20]

Appropriately enough, Hobbes had found his anarchy, or state of nature, existing in his own time among 'the savage people in many places of *America*', his Indians being Jungian ancestors of Personville's citizens. In Hobbes's often-quoted description, the life of man in such a state is 'solitary, poore, nasty, brutish, and short', much like life in Personville (the Op, among others, helping to fulfil the last condition). However, Hobbes insists that under these conditions 'there is no place for Industry; because the fruit thereof is uncertain'.[21] By contrast, Hammett visualises a society in which Hobbesian war or chronic insecurity ('the nature of War, consisteth not in actuall fighting; but in the known disposition thereto') is compatible with flourishing industry. Smelters' stacks dominate the skyline of Personville, and most of the population – with the partial exception of the gangsters and the police – work for Elihu Willsson's enterprises. But the gangsters are themselves a manufacturing and service industry, supplying liquor, gambling, and cheap stolen goods to the citizens. It is a commonplace of the period that 'the gangster, in his perfected and organized form, was the businessman as the businessman wished to be but dared not be, without restrictions or aims but those of power alone'.[22] In Personville the restrictions are forgotten, and businessmen and gangster have become indistinguishable. When four of Pete the Finn's men are killed in a raid on his liquor warehouse, Pete shrugs off their deaths: 'they get paid for taking chances'. He is an employer in a *laissez-faire* economy whose responsibility to his employees is limited to paying them wages. Hammett emphasises the victims' worker status: they are 'swarthy foreign-looking men in laborers' clothes', cheap immigrant labour exploited by a fellow immigrant who has made good in capitalist, criminous America. (The Op, whose many hostilities include an instinctive xenophobia, describes them as 'some dagoes'.) Elihu Willsson, by virtue of his business and political interests, claims to be more respectable than his gangster associates (he can now afford to hire his violence). However, though 'not exactly their brand of cut-throat', he is a self-made man with a questionable past. As he cheerfully confesses to the Op, 'if I hadn't been a pirate I'd still be working for the Anaconda for wages, and there'd be no Personville Mining Corporation' (p. 140). In fact, Willsson has not reformed: he has only become old, sick and frightened.

Perhaps Hammett sees Willsson's condition as that of American capitalism, for the imaginative reach of the novel embraces not only Personville but the whole of America. In the first of his drug-induced dreams in chapter 21 the Op hunts a woman through the named streets of a number of American cities – Baltimore, Denver, Cleveland, Dallas, Boston, Louisville, New York, Jacksonville, El Paso, Detroit, and Rocky Mount, North Carolina. In case it should still not be clear that Personville contains these and all other American cities, the Op later remembers his dream when walking for the last time to Elihu Willsson's house: 'I must have walked as many streets as I did in my dreams.'

III

The Op's commission empowers him to investigate 'crime and political corruption in Personville'. There is no doubting the thoroughness of his investigation of the city's crime, but local politics remain very much in the background. 'I'm told that the mayor and the governor are both pieces of your property', says the Op dismissively to Willsson, and neither official plays any part in the story. As for wider political issues, the novel reflects contemporary concern with proletarian unrest (it can, indeed, be read as the history of the consequences of a strike); but its political distinctions are crude and scarcely more than epithets. Bill Quint the labour organiser is described by Albury as 'that radical chap' and by the Op as 'the radical fellow' – a contemptuous, patronising label. Quint himself refers to Donald Willsson as a 'lousy liberal', presumably because of the murdered man's privileged background, and because his newspaper campaign had been for reform rather than revolution.

Hoping to get information out of Quint, the Op falsely identifies himself as a seaman and a 'member in good standing of the Industrial Workers of the World', with influence at IWW headquarters in Chicago. Quint responds like a private entrepreneur: 'Hell with Chi! I run 'em here.' Union solidarity is evidently as precarious as the gangster alliance. The Op knows that Quint 'considered it his duty to get the low-down on me, and to not let himself be pumped about radical affairs while he was doing it' (p. 8); but it is the Op who extracts more from their conversation. When it suits him, he will claim to be a unionist, just as he later claims to be on side with some of the gangsters. In his opportunistic manipulation of the factions in Personville the Op sees unionism as merely one of those factions, and probably the least important. Organised labour has failed Personville in the past, when the strike collapsed, and the novel never suggests that it can be of any help to the community. After the third chapter Quint drops out of the action, and much later he is mentioned as having slipped quietly out of town, 'leaving no forwarding address'. (Another possible variety of salvation is rejected even more briefly and contemptuously. When the Op is in a lighted hotel room, dodging bullets from across the street, he smashes the light bulb by throwing a Gideon Bible at it. So much for religion in Personville.)

This is the extent of explicit politics in *Red Harvest*, probably as much as the narrator could plausibly deliver, and as much as the text could readily bear without becoming more of a social tract than a hard-boiled thriller. Implicitly, the novel is much richer in political content. The conviction that crime, law enforcement,

Perhaps the eventual attraction of Communism for Hammett was that it claimed to provide the explanation and the cure.

Notes

1. The most important accounts of Hammett's life are William F. Nolan's two studies, *Dashiell Hammett: A Casebook* (Santa Barbara, Calif.: McNally and Loftin, 1969) and *Dashiell Hammett: A Life at the Edge* (London: Arthur Barker, 1983); but reference should also be made to Richard Layman, *Shadow Man: The Life of Dashiell Hammett* (New York: Harcourt Brace Jovanovich, 1981), and Diane Johnson, *The Life of Dashiell Hammett* (London: Chatto and Windus, 1984).

2. On Pinkerton see William Ruehlmann, *Saint with a Gun: The Unlawful American Private Eye* (New York: New York University Press, 1974) pp. 23–31.

3. Dashiell Hammett, *The Big Knockover: Selected Stories and Short Novels*, ed. and with an introduction by Lillian Hellman (New York: Vintage Books, 1972) p. x.

4. Ibid., pp. 115, 132.

5. The Op travels to Mexico in 'The Golden Horseshoe' – *The Continental Op* (New York: Random House, 1974) pp. 41–81; and to the fictional Balkan republic of Muravia in 'This King Business' – *The Big Knockover*, pp. 115–72.

6. Hammett, *The Big Knockover*, p. 34.

7. Norman Mailer, *Miami and the Siege of Chicago* (London: Weidenfeld and Nicolson, 1968) p. 164.

8. Hammett, *The Big Knockover*, p. 388; 'Death on Pine Street' in *The Continental Op* (New York: Lawrence E. Spivak, 1949) p. 54.

9. Lillian Hellman, *Scoundrel Time*, with an introduction by Garry Wills (Boston, Mass.: Little, Brown, 1976) p. 32.

10. Hammett, *The Big Knockover*, pp. 173, 177, 184, 190.

11. Ibid., p. 188.

12. Ibid., pp. 188–9.

13. Ibid., pp. 3–4.

14. Ibid., p. 33.

15. Page references relate to Dashiell Hammett, *Red Harvest* (New York: Vintage Books, 1972). All quotations from the novel are from this edition.

16. Hammett had already used this type of plot in 'Corkscrew' (*Black Mask*, Sep 1925), where a private murder causes several hostile factions in a lawless Arizona town to destroy each other, helped by the Op.

17. James D. Horan, *The Pinkertons* (1967), quoted in Ruehlmann, *Saint with a Gun*, p. 24.

18. Ruehlmann, *Saint with a Gun*, p. 67.

19. Philip Durham, 'The *Black Mask* School', in David Madden (ed.),

Tough Guy Writers of the Thirties (Carbondale: Southern Illinois University Press, 1968) p. 51.

20. Steven Marcus, 'Dashiell Hammett and the Continental Op', in *Representations: Essays on Literature and Society* (New York: Random House, 1976) pp. 325–6.
21. Thomas Hobbes, *Leviathan*, xiii.
22. Elizabeth Stevenson, *The American 1920s: Babbitts and Bohemians* (New York: Collier, 1970) P. 143.
23. Raymond Chandler, *The Simple Art of Murder* (London: Hamish Hamilton, 1950) p. 333.
24. William L. Chenery, *The Century*, 1924; quoted as epigraph to Paul M. Angle, *Resort to Violence: A Chapter in American Lawlessness* (London: Bodley Head, 1954).

6

'A Hard Cheerfulness': An Introduction to Raymond Chandler

STEPHEN KNIGHT

I lay on my back on a bed in a waterfront hotel and waited for it to get dark. It was a small front room with a hard bed and a mattress slightly thicker than the cotton blanket that covered it. A spring underneath me was broken and stuck into the left side of my back. I lay there and let it prod me. . . .

I thought of lots of things. It got darker. The glare of the red neon sign spread farther and farther across the ceiling. I sat up on the bed and put my feet on the floor and rubbed the back of my neck.

I got up on my feet and went over to the bowl in the corner and threw cold water on my face. After a little while I felt a little better, but very little. I needed a drink, I needed a lot of life insurance, I needed a vacation, I needed a home in the country. What I had was a coat, a hat and a gun. I put them on and went out of the room.

In this passage from *Farewell, My Lovely* Chandler gives his version of that major figure in twentieth-century folklore, the private eye. Philip Marlowe has just gone through a set of painful experiences while trying to comprehend some puzzling events and crimes. Alone, tired and gloomy, he still pulls himself together and acts when he must. He has none of the comforts of ordinary life, just those three symbols of the private eye – the trilby hat, the trenchcoat and the ready gun. He is brave, enduring, and knowing as well; he sees right through human hypocrisy; as a result he is distinctly cynical in tone.

As with all heroes of story, the acts, words and thoughts of the private eye can be examined to reveal the fears and hopes of those who find him a satisfying and comforting figure. Even within private-eye fiction, the hero and his tasks can mean surprisingly different things, imply quite different structures of problems and solutions, and so indicate radically different audiences. Mickey Spillane's violent and simplistic novels assure their readers that the threats posed by degenerates, Communists and women can only be contained by a type of vigilante violence. At the opposite extreme, Ross Macdonald's novels trace crime to environmental and family disturbance, and offer treatment as a solution. Raymond Chandler provides a different pattern, in fact one of considerable complexity, with its own central audience. But, before analysing the novels in those terms, it will be helpful to say something about the author and how he came to write private-eye stories.

Raymond Chandler was born in Chicago in 1888, but when he was seven his parents separated and he and his mother (herself of Irish origin) went to live in London with her mother and sister. Chandler's uncle sent him to Dulwich College, and from there he went to a post in the Civil Service. Already he had literary inclinations; after promptly leaving the bureaucracy in 1908, he wrote for several quite prestigious London literary magazines, publishing poems, reviews and essays. At that stage it seems, looking backwards, as if a sensitive young poet and belle-lettrist was emerging. But Chandler turned away from that possibility and went back to America in 1912. It has never become clear why he did so. In later comments he said he found English life oppressive, but he did not feel strongly American at that time. It may simply be that, if he had not returned then, he would have lost his American citizenship.

Whatever the reason, arrival in America brought a new kind of life for Chandler. He eventually found work as a bookkeeper in a small company. A business career was interrupted during the war, when he served in the trenches with a Canadian regiment. Apparently that was a grim experience, but it only surfaces in his work briefly and much later, through Terry Lennox in *The Long Goodbye*, and then the feelings are displaced to the Second World War; it may be, though, that the recurrent scenes of losing consciousness in Chandler's work owe something to his experience of being buried in a trench.

Back in America his business life went on till 1932. He became an accountant and then a senior executive with an oil-producing company in Los Angeles. Life was apparently not simple or easy. He tried to write, but had no success. He drank a lot and continually argued with people. In 1924 he married Cissy Chandler. She was twice divorced and twenty years older than her husband, but this should not suggest a mother figure: she was sprightly and attractive; they shared restless temperaments. Chandler's later comments suggest a blissful married life, but his biographer, Frank MacShane, records various tales of domestic uproar and sexual escapades by Chandler.[1] It was his work life, though, that provided the break which led to a literary career.

In 1932 Chandler parted company with the oil firm, on rather bad terms, and was out of work. He had some savings, friends provided casual jobs and support, and he now decided to make real his long-term ambition to be a writer. He had decided that the newly developed tough-guy private-eye stories were his métier. Written by men such as Dashiell Hammett and Erle Stanley Gardner, they were appearing in 'pulp' magazines, printed on cheap wood-pulp paper. Their voice attracted him: earlier on in Britain he had written in an elaborate, consciously literary style. But the clipped, colloquial tone of these writers, like that of Hemingway, seemed to Chandler the real voice of the America he knew. He found their topics equally real. Far from the artificialities of Agatha Christie and the British school of crime writers, Hammett, in particular, wrote about urban corruption, showing how big business and gangsters were mutually involved in running cities for profit. The terse style and the realistic themes were Chandler's starting-point, and he gave Hammett full credit.[2] But in some ways the relation with Hammett has been overstressed, because Chandler developed his style and themes away from Hammett's patterns. Hammett finished publishing before Chandler started, and they met rarely: it was not a continuing influence. Chandler also studied Erle Stanley Gardner closely; he admired his plotting, especially the even, calm way in which he set out unlikely events and intricate action. But, here too, it was only a start. Chandler created his own plot patterns and his own attitudes to action when he moved up from short stories to the extended length of the novel.

This was the crucial event in shaping his work, in developing the special Chandler characteristics that are so well known and so widely imitated. The change appeared in 1939, when he published *The Big Sleep*. It was based on two previously published short stories, with additional material, and it sold 10,000 copies in the first year, a clear but not huge success. The publishers were eager for another, and Chandler produced *Farwell, My Lovely*, which came out in 1940. This adapted three short stories, and they were interwoven more skilfully than in *The Big Sleep*, where the joins had shown rather clearly. At the same time Chandler was moulding some other stories into *The Lady in The Lake*, but this was not finished and published till 1943, after he completed *The High Window*. That was an entirely new story and seems to reveal Chandler's difficulty in inventing new material – already clear in his habit of cannibalising stories for novels. *The High Window* manages to be both rather contrived and rather dull, and Chandler felt it was his poorest work. He considered *The Big Sleep* lively, but strained in technique and emotion. *The Lady in the Lake* he thought well of, and he was quite sure that *Farewell, My Lovely* was his best book. Many people have agreed with that opinion as well as the others. Edmund Wilson, the American heavyweight champion of book-reviewing, hated crime fiction, but had to admit that *Farewell, My Lovely* was at least worth reading.[3]

Although Chandler had by the early forties won considerable success with critics and with readers, he was still not selling in enormous numbers. It is hardly surprising that he was attracted by the great Californian money-trap for writers. He went to work in Hollywood in 1943 and stayed there, on and off, for some five years. The contact between the irritable, witty writer and the crazy dream-machine produced a lot of friction and some sparks – Chandler has sharp comments in some letters and essays. But it was never very productive for him in creative terms. He worked on famous films such as *Double Indemnity* and *Strangers on a Train* but was not at all pleased with the results, and it is not clear how much he contributed to their success. He wrote some screenplays, but none were outstanding. *The Blue Dahlia* is well known, but the best of them, *Playback*, was never filmed and appeared much later as a novel. Chandler, like Hammett, had great influence on Hollywood, but it was secondary, not made in person: they provided plots and characters that other writers and directors made powerful on the screen, and they gave a model of melodramatic action and tough dialogue that determined the development of what the admiring French call *le film noir*. This aspect of the novels has been brought out by Frederic Jameson in one of the few searching essays on the Chandler's work.[4]

He earned a lot of money in those five Hollywood years, but was mostly uncomfortable. He found it unreal and phony, as literary people usually do. More interestingly, he was defeated by the system: he felt his own work was lost, his personality swamped, in the collective practice of film-making. There were no private rights for the private eye and his author.

The novel he produced in 1949, *The Little Sister*, uses a Hollywood setting and lays more emotive stress on Hollywood phonies and hypocrisy than is good for the plotting. Chandler felt the book was bad-tempered, and it is. He also said 'the writing is of incomparable brilliance but something has went wrong with the story'.[5] The plot is creaky, but the comment is more revealing than that. It points to Chandler's awareness of his 'good writing' – and, in the ironic 'has went', his defensiveness about it. Chandler was aware, and critics kept him aware, of his power to write with insight and style which pointed towards the 'real novel' rather than a mere crime story. He was always edgy about this, sometimes planning to move out of crime writing altogether, but more often and more decisively feeling that the crime novel could be just as valid as any other fiction. His next book was his major bid to produce something that was at once a real novel and a crime story. *The Long Goodbye* came out in 1953.

By this time Chandler was often out of sorts and unable to work. His own health was poor; his wife was now old and very ill, and he was extremely upset when she died in 1954. But he worked with great care on *The Long Goodbye*, his longest book and in many ways the most direct statement of his attitudes to crime, to society, to men and women. Some people have found it too direct, and have complained about its moralism and sentimentality. They are obviously happier to respond to Chandler's sentiment and morality when it is euphemised, made more acceptable and quasi-realist by the tough action and talk of the other novels. But Marlowe and Chandler have not gone soft: they are just less guarded about their attitudes. In general the book was a great success, and Chandler was by now a distinguished figure, well known in many countries, honoured in America and especially so in Britain.

After his wife's death he travelled a good deal, drank a fair amount, but was not happy. There was a notorious bungled suicide attempt and threats of others. But he still had his moments with friends, women and drink. He took special pleasure in shocking the somewhat self-important cultural folk who gathered round him when he visited London – they have carefully recorded their humiliations by the great man.[6] But he was still sick and alone a lot of the time. Writing was hard for him, and intermittent, but he did finally publish *Playback*, the old film script, as a novel. This work has almost uniformly been condemned. It is much shorter than the others, and so is called thinner. But it has really been criticised because it is so different from the others – this stems from the fact that as a script it was written without Marlowe and set in Vancouver. The hero and the Los Angeles setting are the two major dynamic features of the other novels, and this story lacks the issues and the tensions realised through them. But, although *Playback* shows traces of tiredness and self-indulgence here and there, it also lacks some of the touchy neurosis of the other novels, especially towards women, and it has been much underrated. By any other author it would be an outstanding novel, and is a remarkable achievement for an old and often sick man.

Chandler died in 1959. He was celebrated, widely described as a 'good novelist', not just a crime writer. He is often regarded as the doyen of crime writers, the most subtle and searching of them, the finest stylist. The interesting thing is that he has never been a huge seller. It took a long time for a Chandler novel to sell a million copies. Spillane, Gardner and Christie have awed the literary world by their stunning sales figures. But Chandler's reputation is different and has a different source. It comes from the fact that those who enjoyed him most were those who had a powerful voice in cultural media, opinion-makers such as the film-reviewers in the London Sunday heavies, writers such as Stephen Spender and W. H. Auden, and cultural journalists such as Anthony Boucher, the dean of American crime-reviewers. The relatively small sales and the high cultural status are related; their causes converge in the central audience that Chandler appealed to. To see why this is, to expose the full pattern of meaning in Chandler's novels, it is necessary to look closely at the patterns of content and of form in the six related books – that is, all but *Playback*, the aberrant one.[7]

The first thing to examine is the central character. Each novel is told in the first person by the same man, Philip Marlowe. Chandler had a good deal to say about him on various occasions. In the most famous discussion of his hero, he talks first of all about the world he presents in his books, and then goes on to characterise this Philip Marlowe:

> down these mean streets a man must go who is not himself mean, who is neither tarnished nor afraid. The detective in this kind of story must be such a man. He is the hero, he is everything. He must be a complete man and a common man and yet an unusual man. He must be, to use a rather weathered phrase, a man of honour, by instinct, by inevitability, without thought of it, and certainly without saying it. He must be the best man in his world and a good enough man for any world. . . .
>
> The story is this man's adventure in search of a hidden truth and it would be no adventure if it did not happen to a man fit for adventure. He has a range of awareness that startles you, but it belongs to him by right, because it belongs to the world he lives in. If there were enough like him, I think the world would be a very safe place to live in, and yet not too dull to be worth living in.[8]

The action of the novel tells us a good deal more about the hero than that description; in particular the action will define what he fears, and what tools, what values he employs against those fears. Chandler's statement about Marlowe suggests that social corruption is what the hero fights and that freedom, democracy might be the truth he seeks. That is not really so, and the hero is not as romantically admirable as his description suggests. Chandler's official notion of what he did and the actual operations of his creative imagination are quite separate. To see this it is best to look first at the hero, and then go on to the threats he faces and how he handles them.

The hero's name is interesting. The same figure appears in all the early short stories with varying names, but on his very first appearance, in 'Blackmailers Don't Shoot', he is called 'Mallory'. That points to the model behind the figure. Sir Thomas Malory's *Le Morte Darthur*, the classic English account of King Arthur's knights, was well known when Chandler was young; Ernest Rhys's cheap Everyman edition came out in 1906. Chandler's hero is by implication a knight-errant, riding around to defeat villains and rescue the distressed.[9] Marlowe is merely a coded version of the name. The fact that it is a version of the name of the *author* of knight-errant stories suggests that Chandler identifies strongly with the character. There is little doubt this is so, and it may extend to Chandler's own half-British, half-American character. A number of US-based critics have remarked that 'Philip Marlowe' is a very British-sounding name – and that the final 'e' in 'Marlowe' stresses the point in spelling.

Marlowe's personal characteristics and attitudes hardly change through the novels and they are important to his overall impact. He lives alone, in rented flats or houses. He works alone, in a cheap, comfortless office. He drinks and smokes a lot: a single, masculine life style. He is choosy about his work, never showing much interest in money. In general, he has dropped right out of the normal family and financial patterns of modern culture.

He even has no girl friends. He quite likes professional, competent women with an apparently reduced sexuality, such as Anne O'Riordan in *Farewell, My Lovely* or Adrienne Fromsett in *The Lady in the Lake*, but he rapidly leaves when Anne offers him her favours. He feels tenderly towards downtrodden mousy girls such as Merle Davis in *The High Window*, and Orfamay Quest, the Little Sister herself (but he is quite wrong about her, and that is predicted when she kisses him in the first scene). He is distinctly bothered by overt sexual advances, as from Carmen Sternwood in *The Big Sleep* and Dolores Gonzalez in *The Little Sister*. One of the odd features of *Playback* is that Marlowe has two casual and undisturbing sexual encounters, one with his rather plain client, the other with an efficient and aggressive secretary, so breaking two old taboos in a row.

As far as men go, Marlowe is very hostile if they are effeminate. Arthur Geiger in *The Big Sleep* and Lindsay Marriott in *Farewell, My Lovely* are clearly homosexual and they both die grotesquely, immediately after being examined with disfavour by Marlowe. Intriguingly,he also dislikes men who are fully dependent on women, gigolos such as Chris Lavery in *The Lady in the Lake* and Louis Vannier in *The High Window*. They also die in ugly ways. Evidently, feminine power in or over men is not enjoyed at all, and sexual unease comes strongly through all Marlowe's encounters with men and women. None of these feelings, it is interesting to notice, is in the least related to the unveiling of urban corruption.

The only other people Marlowe really dislikes are the evil doctors who keep turning up to fill him with drugs or restrain him in their barred-window clinics. He is not fond of corrupt police, such as the well-named Chief Wax in *Farewell, My Lovely*, but he does deal with them on a fairly even basis. There is even some sympathy for heavy-handed corrupt police such as Hemingway in *Farewell, My Lovely* and Delgarmo in *The Lady in the Lake*. Marlowe positively likes big fatherly police – Jim Patton in *The Lady in the Lake* and Jesse Breeze in *The High Window*, for example.

As a view of professional corruption this is interesting, and limited. Doctors are more disturbing than police, as if the hero is more perturbed by those who can get to his body in some way – sexy women who make him weaken, rich women who can buy men, homosexuals who can also be seductive, doctors who have their own ways of controlling him against his will. The perceived threat is personal, not social. This individualist response is confirmed when Marlowe gets on rather well with the gangsters he meets. He does find some hitmen revolting – for instance, Lash Canino and Joseph P. Toad in *The Big Sleep* and *The Little Sister* respectively – but they threaten him personally. The big bosses turn out to be rather presentable and decent men: Eddie Mars in *The Big Sleep* is slightly ominous but civil enough to Marlowe. Laird Brunette in *Farewell, My Lovely* is friendly and helpful, responding to Marlowe's honourable character. Alex Morny in *The High Window* is quite a gentleman, himself vexed with a sexy wife, and Marlowe lets him get away with murder. The mobsters in *The Long Goodbye* are loyal friends to Terry Lennox. Gangsters, and the senior police, are presented frequently as businessmen, and, as Captain Gregory makes clear in *The Big Sleep*, this exculpates the gangsters; it does *not* imply, as it might with Hammett, that all businessmen are gangsters. So much for the fearless exposure of corruption that Chandler himself implied he gave – and there is no clear sign of corruption among judges, lawyers, bureaucrats, newspaper editors.

Marlowe does show some distaste for the rich, but he sees them merely as lifeless, like Mr Grayle in *The Big Sleep* and Harlan Potter in *The Long Goodbye*, or moribund, like General Sternwood in *The Big Sleep*, who is admirable in that he was vigorous in the past. Marlowe finds the great houses of the rich mostly like prisons, and pities their inmates rather than hating exploitation in the way that Hammett did. Chandler's lack of any real critique of Californian wealth is probed in an essay by Bernard Sharratt.[10] At the same time there is no real pity for the poor: they are presented with some distaste as dirty, without vitality. And there are not many of them: some poor whites appear, but, as with Erle Stanley Gardner,

Chandler's southern California contains very few blacks and almost no Mexicans at all. Throughout these encounters collective concepts such as class and race are quite absent; the responses are entirely personal and instinctively negative, valuing only the hero's position and attitudes. A couple of characters he does admire are the failed private detectives Harry Jones in *The Big Sleep* and George Phillips in *The High Window*. They are small-time and hardly competent, but they did their best to be good detectives and are at least honest men. It is the dishonesty of his friend Terry Lennox that so disappoints him in *The Long Goodbye*.

Some positive attitudes do offset Marlowe's lengthy series of negative and often distinctly questionable attitudes. He is very persevering; he covers the city at all hours in his quest for solutions. There is a tremendous number of addresses in Chandler, and most chapters begin with one. Chandler himself was forever moving houses, and there may be a direct link – restless, rootless figures looking for something. Marlowe is also firmly moral as well as stubbornly busy. He will not do divorce work and he only covers up crimes on his client's behalf if he thinks it is proper to do so. In fact his morality is his own: he is not even really for hire in the sense of being at the client's disposal. He starts on a case, then follows his nose. Independence and insubordination are deep-seated characteristics and the investigation that is the major part of each novel is never what his client initially asks for. Marlowe largely makes his own case to investigate: he is a private detective in being outside the police, but he is also a *really* private eye, choosing what he wants to look at. The positive values, as well as the negative features of Marlowe, centre on the separate individual, who needs to be strong, active, defended against dangers and temptations.

Not only is Marlowe independent and incorruptible; he is also rather intelligent, cultured and sensitive. Playing chess against himself is the recurrent token of this, a splendidly isolative image. Now and then he throws in literary references to assert his special qualities. But the dominant way of communicating this special intelligence and insight is Marlowe's analysing description of the people and places he encounters. The force and meaning of the character are very much created by Marlowe's style, or rather his styles. They indicate the range of awareness Chandler spoke about in his hero, the crucial mixture of sensitivity and toughness that is dramatised in Marlowe's speaking voice and offered as a response to the world. Chandler eludes the simplicities of a merely tough heroic style. Marlowe can be genuinely sensitive and observant. This happens especially when he is waiting to act, or when he is doing nothing and the plot will soon bring him a client, a threat, some action. Then he watches, listens, responds in sharp and sensitive ways to the world about him. In these passages the material is very fluently and sensitively written: the intelligence of the hero is irrestible, impressive. But it is not allowed to be romantic, unqualified sensitivity: primarily it is expressed in irony, cynicism – the trace of poetry in Marlowe has a negative poetic. Only in the sea and the mountains beyond Los Angeles does Marlowe find anything untouched by human and urban blight, and then he is aware all the time of the contrast with his real environment, so painfully perceived.

If Marlowe is ironically guarded in his meditations, shared only by the audience, it is not surprising that he is much more negative and defensive in the language he shares with other characters. In fact the voice of Marlowe's reverie, both subtle and ironic, is quite different from the voice he uses to other characters. When speaking to the reader his sensitive humanity shows through, however much he ironically protects it. But to the people he meets in the action he is uniformly tough and insensitive: to them he is only witty in ways that are aggressive, clipped, unimaginative, even relentless. In fact a lot of the time Marlowe says little; he just responds with an ironic grin and lets the other person flounder. The style of the novels, that is, creates a double man whose full humanity is only released in private reverie, speaking to his literary audience. His working life and his encounters with people are arid and painful; if they are seductively pleasant, his language shows that there is something wrong with the person, or at least that nothing can come of the encounter, as with Anne O'Riordan in *The Big Sleep* or Mavis Weld in *The Little Sister*.

Language for Marlowe is both a defensive tool against others and a self-realisation in the privacy of his mind and his narrative. The great powers of insight and persuasion that he privately possesses are not outwardly released to make him into a writer, a lawyer, a politician. The striking thing about Marlowe's work is that it does not employ the inner talents he reveals to us: a gulf is set between the self and the work. The pattern that is evolved in language for the novels is the alienation of the self, the privatised world of the individual, a structure where the person has a rich inner life and a defensive, even hostile, exterior, unable to share with others the humanity which is felt and privately enjoyed.

That is a powerful contemporary image, of course. But it is not charted only in style and in the hero's response to people. The same pattern is realised in the action of the novels, because Chandler constructs his own plot patterns, and they too spiral in towards the anxious, alienated inner self.

To see this, it is necessary to stress the way in which Chandler developed away from Hammett. The plot patterns he took from him, and used fairly straight in the short stories, told how a cool-eyed and incorruptible figure can discover and even frustrate the corrupt schemes of those who run modern cities: industrialists, politicians, lawyers, editors – gangsters above all. This forcefully social pattern has a clear view of an oppressive capitalist and criminal system, but in an important way it is not socialist: it has no social or collective positive values. Even Hammett uses a single investigator and offers no organised opposition to the enemies he identifies. Perhaps that is why a steady drift into non-political individualism occurs in Hammett's later novels, in spite of his radical views.

Chandler certainly valued the socially conscious and corruption-conscious approach and he did offer Marlowe as a crusader against urban crime. The general idea is still held about Chandler's novels that they show the enemies out there, capitalistic, bureaucratic, criminal, all operating against us. There are gangsters, tough cops and crooked professionals in Chandler's novels, but it has already become clear through discussing Marlowe's attitudes to people that those figures are not the major disturbing force in the novels. It is those who are personally close to Marlowe who cause him trouble; they can excite and so betray him. The plot of the novels, the crime and its detection all assert that these are the people who really cause criminal disorder; these are the ones you need to detect at their villainous work.

Essentially the novels have double plots. There is an outer structure where what has gone wrong is loosely associated with corruption, gangsters, professional crime. This is the plot that is offered at first, and so a Hammett-type novel about corruption seems under way – blackmailers and racketeers in *The Big Sleep*, jewel gangs and gangsters in *Farewell, My Lovely*, forgers and gambling in *The High Window*, police corruption and drug doctors in *The Lady in the Lake*, gangsters and Hollywood hypocrisy in *The*

Little Sister, racketeers and high-life corruption in *The Long Goodbye*. But none of these people or patterns turns out really to have been behind the central crime, and they fade from the action as the inner, personalised plot is steadily revealed, as the actual betrayer and killer becomes exposed.

In *The Big Sleep* the outer and inner plots come from two different short stories, but the other novels still have this double pattern. It is obviously of central importance. The gangster material does become more and more perfunctory, but there always remains an outer, public and socially attuned area of operation with a bogus problem and a suggested solution. They fall away, and the gangsters actually turn out to have been themselves employed by the agent of the inner plot, the betraying, personally threatening force that Marlowe identifies and is himself threatened by. To see how this works, to establish the crucial crimes and criminals, here is an analysis of *Farewell, My Lovely*.

Marlowe accidentally meets Moose Malloy, who is looking for Velma. Marlowe, for no good reason, makes some inquiries about her. Out of the blue he is hired by Lindsay Marriott to help buy back a friend's stolen jewels. But, when they go to do this, Marlowe is knocked out and Marriott beaten to death with the same weapon. *Now* Marlowe is hired by the owner of the jewels, Mrs Grayle, to sort things out. There is talk of a jewel gang and organised crime; Marlowe is roughed up by the police, drugged and locked up in two separate hospitals. It seems as if some huge public plot is operating to stop his inquiries. But things turn round: through Mrs Grayle's influence Chief Wax, the most corrupt cop, is helpful. And then Marlowe meets Laird Brunette, the chief gangster, and he is as noble and charming as his name suggests – he has been hiding Malloy from the police and produces him for Marlowe. At the climax all is revealed: Mrs Grayle did everything. She is the elusive Velma; she hired Marlowe through Marriott, knocked out the hero and bashed Marriott to death; she finally shoots Malloy and tries to shoot Marlowe; then she goes away and kills herself in what Marlowe thinks is a moment of conscience. She is beautiful and spurious, charming and deadly: lovely, and very farewellable.

It is not just what happens, but where and how it happens, that reveals the full latent meaning. Mrs Grayle has been more than friendly to Marlowe, ready to betray her aged husband at any time. The final shooting scene takes place in Marlowe's bedroom: he is in pyjamas and Malloy is hiding there. Marlowe has always liked Malloy – they got into the mystery together and they nearly end together. Marriott and Marlowe were also together when they were both attacked, with the same weapon. It is clear that Mrs Grayle's victims are proxies for Marlowe, and it is most interesting that one is big and macho, one distinctly effeminate – apparently two aspects of the hero, expressing his fears that his projected masculinity is frail.

This whole pattern is common in the novels. The villain is consistently a sexy woman who gets very close to the hero; she kills those he likes and dislikes, positive and negative projections of himself. *The High Window* is an exception of a sort: there the villainess has a different sort of relation with her victims and with Marlowe, but still one by which the female threatens the male – as a bogus mother rather than a bogus lover. In making these issues of personal anxiety central, Chandler has come a long way from exposing urban corruption.

Marlowe's detective methods are precisely in line with this pattern of a threat to the private self. He does very little normal detecting: gathering facts about the outer world is not his forte. He is much more passive than that. He does travel about with energy, if not pleasure, but it is to watch, listen, to wait for the truth to come to him. He is as passive as an isolate will be. His passivity is the medium of his vulnerability: not engaging in social interaction or busy objective detection, he is actually pressed in on by the forces he is avoiding. Discovery of the truth seems a reward for his values, enacted as they are by his sheer perseverance.

The threats that destroy the victims and come uncomfortably close to Marlowe are, first, betrayal and, then, death. It is usually said that murder is the central crime of modern fiction because of our period's obsessive individualism. Robbery or shame were the major threats in earlier periods, when family property and honour seemed larger issues than the private life.[11] Chandler certainly takes death seriously as a threat; not only is it the central crime, but in suitably euphemised and sensitive form it stars in most of his titles – *The Big Sleep*, *The Long Goodbye*, *The Lady in the Lake*, *Farewell, My Lovely*. *The High Window* refers to the place where the fatal betrayal and murder has taken place. Only *The Little Sister* avoids death and instead names the central betrayer of relatives and Marlowe.

In general the novels express the fears of the modern, privatised individual, who does not see matters socially or collectively at all, but just fears that those who are closest might not prove trustworthy, that committing yourself is a threat, that true life is in sensitive guarded watchfulness, and that death is a final extinction.

And out there the big city remains. And all the people in it. Style and plot spiral inwards, and that self-absorption and self-protection is an urgent necessity because the novels realise so powerfully the urban jungle that the private individual sees out there, embodying the threats to the self in a concrete, dehumanised image that is easier to hate and dismiss than if its inhabitants were all seen as separate individuals. The city is very real and remains one of the most powerful forces in Chandler's work. The essence of the novels is the dynamic conflict between the one figure and the city, the reification of all the feared others.

Los Angeles was the first great dehumanised urban sprawl, and it remains the archetype. A part of Chandler's power is that he created this new experience of mechanised urban anomie and interpreted it authoritatively for those who suffer it. And, just as he has to work to live, so the hero must live in the city – in 'The Simple Art of Murder', discussing Marlowe and his world, Chandler said, 'It is not a very fragrant world, but it is the world you live in.' He was speaking both as the writer and as the modern citizen, bound like Marlowe to the city, unwillingly but inevitably. It is striking how much of the action takes place at the very edges of the city, by the beach, up against the foothills where the canyons peter out, or even at times in the city's own extensions, in the mountains, at the lakes, out at sea. But Marlowe does not manage to get away from the city: he remains marginal and tied to it as he is to social life. Marlowe is an authentic urban product, just like the alienated intellectual Chandler who wrote the stories and the educated urban individuals who make up his central audience.

There is a lot that can be criticised in Chandler. He comes across as undoubtedly sexist, neurotically prejudiced against women and homosexuals, politically blind to class problems and race conflict in southern California. His work can be sentimental and it can also take the easy way out of a conflict with a slick joke, a neatly turned simile. His plots often ramble, and many of the characters are stereotyped – they almost all talk in the same tough, street-wise way. But these characteristics are authentic to the central presentation; as a fictional creation they are coherent and powerful. The self-conscious, alienated hero *is* narrow in his attitudes and vision, because he is so fearful of others; the plots do ramble, because he does not master experience – it just rolls on before him. He takes verbally slick ways out of problems because his wit protects him from them; he sees almost all the characters alike because they are all equally hostile to him, barring a few downtrodden mice he is able to like.

That is, Chandler's novels are a fully imagined whole, and are an authentic presentation of a real feeling people have had and still have, itself a response to real conditions of living. The tensions and attitudes are natural and dynamic in our period – and the fact that the novels do not solve them, just create and face them, is part of their power. It is important that Marlowe finds no way out, just manages to grin and bear it. He never moves out alone to seek some guru, or to find peace in the wilderness; he never sees suddenly the nuclear-family light, gets married and has children. In fact when he did marry him off, at the end of *Playback*, Chandler ran out of steam to write about him.

For all the sentimentality, bad temper, snide feelings, inhumane simplifications and ideological omissions, the last impression is of a figure who has not given in, has at least faced up to real modern forces. Marlowe the detective and Chandler the writer are persevering; they keep at it, still quipping, still registering what happens to them. They are at least awake and can still kick, even in Los Angeles, even in the twentieth century. They may be ground down, but they are not yet out; it may not be much of a life, but they are alive. That guardedly positive note was realised at Chandler's imaginative and persuasive best when, in *Farewell, My Lovely*, he described the figure whose portrait hangs on Marlowe's office wall. The description will stand as a last word on Marlowe, and even on Chandler himself:

They had Rembrandt on the calendar that year, a rather smeary self-portrait due to imperfectly registered colour plates. It showed him holding a smeared palette with a dirty thumb and wearing a tam-o'-shanter which wasn't any too clean either. His other hand held a brush poised in the air, as if he might be going to do a little work after a while, if somebody made a down payment. His face was ageing, saggy, full of the disgust of life and the thickening effects of liquor. But it had a hard cheerfulness that I liked, and the eyes were as bright as drops of dew.

Notes

1. Frank MacShane, *The Life of Raymond Chandler* (London: Cape, 1976).
2. Chandler mentions Hammett in several of his letters – see *Selected Letters of Raymond Chandler*, ed. Frank MacShane (London: Cape, 1981); but the firmest statement is in the important essay 'The Simple Art of Murder', repr. in *The Simple Art of Murder* (Boston, Mass.: Houghton Mifflin, 1950) and in *Pearls are a Nuisance* (Harmondsworth: Penguin, 1964), but *not* contained in the British story collection entitled *The Simple Art of Murder* (Harmondsworth: Penguin, 1965).
3. See Edmund Wilson, 'Who Cares Who Killed Roger Ackroyd?', repr. in *Classics and Commercials* (London: Allen and Unwin, 1951).
4. Frederic Jameson, 'On Raymond Chandler', *Southern Review*, 6 (1970) 624–50.
5. In a letter to Hamish Hamilton (*Selected Letters*, p. 231).
6. See the essays by Dilys Powell, Natasha Spender and Michael Gilbert in *The World of Raymond Chandler*, ed. M. Gross (London: Weidenfeld and Nicolson, 1977).
7. Some of the following points are made in greater detail in the discussion of *Farewell, My Lovely*, in my book *Form and Ideology in Crime Fiction* (London: Macmillan, 1980; Bloomington: Indiana University Press, 1981) ch. 5.
8. In 'The Simple Art of Murder' (see n. 2).
9. This aspect of Marlowe is brought out most fully (and most sentimentally) by Philip Durham in *Down These Mean Streets a Man Must Go: Raymond Chandler's Knight* (Durham, NC: University of North Carolina Press, 1963).
10. See Bernard Sharratt, 'Question 6: Raymond Chandler, *The Big Sleep*', in *Reading Relations: Structures of Literary Production* (Brighton: Harvester, 1982).
11. This pattern is discussed in *Form and Ideology in Crime Fiction*, ch. 1.

7

Sexuality, Guilt and Detection: Tension between History and Suspense

RICHARD BRADBURY

'Two things may be said of Cain with great assurance: nothing he ever wrote was completely outside the category of trash; in spite of the ultimate cheapness of his novels, an inordinate number of intelligent and fully literate people read him.'[1] This obvious inability to come to terms with what are clearly seen as two contradictory elements in Cain's writing supplies my starting-point. It is clear that Frohock's prescriptive model for literature, in which the assumed concerns of the 'intelligent and fully literate' reader occupy a realm different from those of the common reader (whose appetites may be satisfied by 'trash'), is under attack. Julian Symons's assertion of Hemingway's stylistic debt to Hammett, Gide's admiration for the latter, and the growing critical machinery attempting to close the gap between 'popular' and 'high' culture – which has recently revealed Chekhov as the author of a crime novel as well as highly regarded plays and stories – testify to this development. In this environment, Cain's writing can be reassessed – because, of course, 'trash' and 'ultimate cheapness' are code words indicating an unhesitating, if ambivalent, confrontation with sexuality and violence in an almost completely amoral universe.

The dominant paradigm for the crime novel is the gradual explication, by rational inquiry or psychological insight, of initial mystery by an observer. Whether the text is by Chandler or Christie, it moves towards an understanding of events by remaining more or less detached from the perpetrator's motivation. At the moment immediately before the narrative closure, the action is explained and the criminal is revealed. But this is always within an apparently objective descriptive framework, and the effect of this is to distance the reader from the unfolding of the stimuli which have produced the central actions. This makes possible the recuperation of a normality which pre-existed the events of the text, thereby portraying what has happened as deviant.

James M. Cain's contribution to the writing of crime fiction was to recognise the potential afforded by writing from within the 'criminal's' perspective. This is the formal coup of *The Postman Always Rings Twice, Double Indemnity,* and *The Butterfly*: at the end of these three texts the reader 'discovers' that what he or she has been reading is the transcription of a confession. The possibilities that this opened up were recognised, most famously, by Albert Camus when he acknowledged his debt to *The Postman Always Rings Twice* in the writing of *L'Etranger*. Cain's writing makes possible an examination of motivation more convincing, precisely because it is internalised, than the revelation necessary to bring to a conclusion a work written from the investigator's point of view. The reader, then, can discard the more or less interesting question, 'who dunnit?' and replace this with an attention directed towards a demonstration of the reasons behind the act. At the same time, the first-person narrative eliminates the possibility of a return to normality because all three of these novels conclude, explicitly or implicitly, with the death of the author. There is no informing intelligence within the text which returns the reader to the realm of external and rational explanation. It is, clearly, this absence of any sense of a privileged normality which attracted Camus to Cain's work. And Robbe-Grillet's comment on the mechanisms whereby Camus achieves this could equally well be applied to Cain's writing: 'Just change the tenses of the verbs very slightly, replace the first person ... by the ordinary third person of the past definite, and Camus's universe immediately disappears, together with the whole interest of his book.'[2] For Cain's world in the Depression-year novels is a world of essentially 'homely' characters plunged into a material deprivation which enforces the need for extreme action in order to survive in a fashion anything like that to which they are accustomed. It is a world in which the quintessentially American posture of individual effort being rewarded with security has been shattered by the economic collapse. And thus it is as a world in which the restitution of normality at the end of any single text can only appear as a bad joke.

And, although he shows no direct interest in the political consequences of the Wall Street crash, dismissing as he does the thirties novels of social protest as based on a theme which is 'a dead seed for a novelist', the spectres of the crisis stalk around the edges of his fiction. Herbert Pierce is ruined by Black Thursday, and the opening description of Frank Chambers makes him a close relative of Tom Joad. The urge for financial gain, for access to the means of acquiring material fulfilment, is welded to the urge for sexual fulfilment. Even in *Mildred Pierce*, the least interesting of the 'five great novels' for the purposes of this essay, Cain has a clear understanding of the interaction between money and sexuality as he charts Mildred's use of both to gain power and success – those two chimeras of the Depression years. This historical period, then, is much more than simply a backdrop to his writing; it is an external fact which shapes the broad contours of the internal action of the text. In this era of material deprivation, the possibility of acquiring money and property acts as a force to drive the characters to extremes of behaviour. Although Freud claimed that money was not a great source of psychological motivation, much American crime fiction of the thirties seems to argue against him. The source of this, in all probability, lies in the naturalist writers of the earlier part of the century – in their identification of the search for financial security and success as an almost sexual desire.

For Cain, this desire for money is always closely allied to sexual desire and violence:

I, so far as I can sense the pattern of my mind, write of the wish that comes true, for some reason a terrifying concept, at least to my imagination. Of course, the wish must really have terror in it: just wanting a drink wouldn't quite be enough. I think my stories have some quality of the opening of a forbidden box, and that it is this, rather than violence, sex, or any of the things usually cited by way of explanation, that gives them the drive so often noted. Their appeal is first to the mind, and the reader is carried along as much by his own realisation that the characters cannot have this particular wish and survive, and his curiosity to see what happens to them, as by the effect on him of incident, dialogue, or character.[3]

Cain's characters open the Pandora's box containing all those things forbidden them by the family as social institution, by the work ethic, or by the notion that peaceful social intercourse is the necessary oil on the wheels of society. The box, of course, contains both the objects of their desire and the Furies which manifest themselves as the opposite, but logical, conclusions of that desire. Frank and Cora murder Nick in order to be together, but this togetherness degenerates into the claustrophobic suspicion that the other is about to confess. This brings them to the brink of discovery and, having avoided that initial revelation by a process they barely understand, they enter into a relationship which parallels and parodies marriage to the point at which pregnancy – the mark of the continuation of the family – causes the accident which is misperceived as a second murder and for which Frank is executed.

Cain is correct when he ascribes the intellectual interest of his fiction to the image of the forbidden, but nevertheless opened, box of wishes. But two other elements are crucial to the formula which produces his work, and these are, most obviously, the violence and sex integral to the working-out of the narrative, and his adoption of the first-person pronoun as the dominant voice. This is not simply personal preference for 'a vividness of speech that goes beyond anything I could invent',[4] despite Cain's assertion that 'my short stories, which were put into the mouth of some character, marched right along, for if I in the third person faltered and stumbled, my characters in the first person knew perfectly well what they had to say'.[5] It is a calculated shift away from the naturalists, in whose work the consistent use of the third person holds desires and actions at a distance as part of a campaign to describe, in quasi-scientific fashion, the social and natural causes of human behaviour.

Mildred Pierce is, arguably, the weakest of the five novels because it does not make use of this stylistic strength. This narrative mode, along with a rigorous avoidance of abstraction and adjectival modification, helped to establish, despite his protestations, Cain as one of the high points of 'hard-boiled' writing; an an exemplar of the 'masculine style' of inter-war writing in the United States. This notion of the masculine style was not only central to the critical language employed to assess this mode of writing during its development, but is also crucially important in any account of Cain's work. It is not simply a matter of linguistic formulation, because this is complementary to a frame of mind, an attitude. The conjunction of Hammett, Hemingway and Cain into a triumvirate

of terse stylists is a given of critical judgement, and it is based on
their mutual assertion of the importance of 'an excellent ear' – on
their ability to make reported speech function as a self-sufficient
bearer of import.

> I thought: Well, why all this 'saying'? With quotes around it,
> would they be gargling it? And so, if I may make a plea to my
> fellow fiction-writers, I should like to say: It is about time this
> convention, this dreary flub-dub that lies within the talent of any
> magazine secretary, was dropped overboard and forgotten. If
> Jake is to warn Harold, 'an ominous glint appearing in his eye', it
> would be a great deal smoother and more entertaining to the
> reader, though I grant you nothing like so easy, to slip a little,
> not too much of course, but just the right subtle amount, of
> ominous glint in the speech.[6]

Beyond this similarity, though, there is a divergence. 'Men without
women' is a convenient and obvious expression of Hemingway's
position and also, to a lesser extent, of Hammett's. But for Cain it is
not. The juxtaposition of expressions of aggressive male sexuality
and violence recurs repeatedly in his writing and is simply stated,
never enclosed within any kind of critical moral framework. And it
would be a mistake to attempt to recruit Cain to a critique of these
patterns: not least because their repeated assertion is crucial to the
narrative paradigm of his novels. Equally well, assertive female
sexuality and female violence are sources of fear for his narrators.
They desire the women around them and, at the same time, have a
fear not only of the consequences of the fulfilled desire, but of the
desire itself. Cora, Phyllis, Kady and Maira are all capable of
producing self-destructive actions from their respective counter-
parts by virtue of their sexual attractions: hence, again, the
juxtapositon of sex with violence and death. Once entrapped by
physical attraction, the male narrators cannot break free even if
they recognise that they are trapped.

> next thing I knew the point of the steel was sticking out the back
> of the sofa, and blood was foaming out of Winston's mouth, and
> she was over him, talking to him, laughing at him, telling him
> the detective was waiting to take him down to hell.
> It flashed over me, that mob at the novilladas, pouring down
> out of the sol, spitting on him, twisting the tail of the dying bull,

kicking at him, spitting on him, and I tried to tell myself I had hooked up with a savage, that it was horrible. It was no use. I wanted to laugh, to cheer, and yell Olé! I knew I was looking at the most magnificent thing I had ever seen in my life.[7]

Before moving on, it is as well to look in some detail at this passage, going beyond the obvious apposition of fear and horror with exhilaration and admiration to examine the precise construction of this picture. Maira has adopted a dominant position above Winston, penetrating his body. Blood, the mark of female sexual activity 'foams' from his body while she laughs at him because he has been 'had'. Jack's response is, clearly, based partly on a relief that the homosexual threat which Winston represents has been removed. But this is combined with a fearful knowledge that, unable to break free for himself, he has had to rely on Maira's action to escape and that, as a result, he is connected to her by a bond which began in sexual attraction and which has now been strengthened by death. The image of the bullfight is, I take it, both an image of primitive violence and also of humiliation and attack – presumably, of the consequences of being acknowledged as homosexual in the machismo-imbued society from which Maira originates. For the (albeit mildly) sexually ambiguous Jack, Maira represents the easily available partner, the dominant partner and an explosive violence. For Cain's narrative technique to operate fully, the text must reveal the levels on which these composite figures operate.

All these figures, though, are rooted in the image of the *femme fatale*, a figure common to the works of the hard-boiled school. She stalks the novels, consistently attempting to lure the protagonist/ narrator into her sphere through a combination of sexual allure and apparent vulnerability. The crucial difference between Cain and (especially) Chandler is that the former's narrators become enmeshed with this female figure, whilst Phillip Marlowe resists her charms. Marlowe's ethical sense and 'shabby aristocrat' code of conduct prevents him from turning a blind eye to her actions in his quest for justice. Cain acknowledges the power of sexuality time and again as his men abandon their morality, and more or less fixed life style, to commit acts of violence and murder in return for monetary gain and/or sexual favours. This difference is most clearly highlighted in Chandler's letter to Blanche Knopf:

James Cain – faugh! Everything he touches smells like a billygoat. He is every kind of writer I detest, a faux naïf, a Proust in greasy overalls, a dirty little boy with a piece of chalk and a board fence and nobody looking. Such people are the offal of literature, not because they write about dirty things, but because they do it in a dirty way. Nothing hard and clean and ventilated. A brothel with a smell of cheap scent in the front parlor and a bucket of slops at the back door.[8]

Leaving aside a symptomatic reading of Chandler's letter (which at the very least would take note of his persistent association of sexuality with smell, dirt and excrement!), it is clear that Chandler's objection to Cain centres on his 'dirty', i.e. amoral, stance. His characters surrender their ethical sense to the pressures of the psyche.

Whilst, in a post-Freudian era, we may acknowledge Cain's recognition of the force of sexuality as more 'realistic' than Chandler's avoidance (at least until the repressed returns as violence in *Playback*), we equally well have to recognise that Cain's model is stereotypical. His women are assertive sexual creatures, whose expressions of sexuality lead to what is clearly presented as evil or perversion. Beyond the responses generated by the times – indeed, at those times when the female characters are furthest from the immediate pressures – they show themselves to be nightmarish or simply unexplainedly perverse. This is most obvious at the end of *Double Indemnity*, when Phyllis is revealed as the image of death:

She's made her face chalk white, with black circles under her eyes and red on her lips and cheeks. She's got that red thing on. It's awful-looking. It's just one big square of red silk that she wraps around her, but it's got no armholes, and her hands look like stumps underneath it when she moves them around. She looks like what came aboard the ship to shoot dice for souls in the Rhyme on the Ancient Mariner.[9]

That she is dressed in red is not accidental, not only because the linguistic formulation reminds me of the iconography of the vagina in fifteenth- and sixteenth-century painting but also because it clearly marks the blood already spilled, the blood about to be spilt, and, perhaps most importantly, that she is still sexually active. For

Walter Huff this is nightmare, which can only be set aside, if at all, by contrition through death. The inference is clear, and is spelled out by the associative stream of images Walter chooses to describe Phyllis. Fulfilled desire leads to violence and, ultimately, to the destruction of the male narrator. Cain accepts sexuality, but it is always accepted as a destructive force. Women are either the passive web in which men entangle themselves, or they are the spider; the 'black widow' which entices the male and then eats it; actively spinning a web in which to trap the man. In both cases, though, sex is the bait which lures them further and further into a procession of events which culminate in destruction.

When this presented through a narrator who is, at best, semi-articulate and self-analytical at only the most rudimentary level, Cain has a narrative structure in which his characters are at the whim of forces they cannot understand. Psychological forces combine with external forces – the end of Prohibition, the intricacies of the legal system – to victimise them. Here, again, Cain has a debt to the naturalists, most pertinently to Dreiser's *an American Tragedy*, in which subconscious desires are projected out into a world of objective, if gratuitous, events. That Clyde Griffiths wishes to kill his pregnant girlfriend, actually does not, but is convicted and executed for her murder anyway, is clearly and bitterly ironic. That Frank Chambers evades conviction for a planned murder, only to be executed for an accidental death just at the moment at which domestic happiness appears as a possibility, is of the same order. But Frank's refusal to accept the role of the subconscious leads him to believe unequivocally that Cora dies accidentally and not that he is, in any way, to blame for her death because he, subconsciously, wished for it.

There's a guy in No. 7 that murdered his brother, and says he didn't really do it, his subconscious did it. I asked him what that meant, and he says you got two selves, one that you know about and the other that you don't know about, because it's subconscious. It shook me up. Did I really do it, and not know it? God Almighty, I can't believe that! I didn't do it! I loved her so, then, I tell you, that I would have died for her! To hell with the subconscious. I don't believe it. It's just a lot of hooey, that this guy thought up so he could fool the judge. You know what you're doing, and you do it. I didn't do it, I know that.[10]

To the very end, he is a victim of his own subconscious – unable to analyse his desires and therefore incapable of escaping their hold. Trapped by his inexplicable (because unexamined) lust for Cora into killing Nick, Frank remains throughout imprisoned in his belief that he understands and can control his behaviour. But because he refuses to acknowledge the existence of the subconscious, even when it generates the emblematic love-making beside the car containing the dead body, he is at its mercy.

What is at issue here is not an analysis of Frank's psyche whereby we can decide to what degree he is guilty of Cora's death, but rather the presentation of the notion that he refuses to accept that he could be to blame in any way. It is for the investigator to judge the connection between desire and action. Frank, as protagonist and author, simply manifests the link.

The same is true of his defencelessness before the machinations of the lawyers and the labyrinths of the legal system. Not understanding how he has avoided conviction for the first crime, he cannot comprehend how it is that he is to be punished for an accident. His protestations of innocence are as nothing before the offered proof that he is 'a mad dog', just as his earlier admission that Nick was murdered was as nothing before Katz's manoeuvrings. His behaviour, and his language, are a small grain caught between the greater stones of the deep structures of his psyche and the superior force of the law.

The inarticulacy, then, of the narrator figures is not merely an adherence to a prevailing stylistic formulation, but also a commitment to a narrative model which 'shows and tells' – but never explains because it cannot explain. Cain's narrative voices present themselves through their actions or through their thoughts about matters external to themselves, but they fall silent at the point of self-analysis. Thus, they offer us as readers the (dubious) voyeuristic and vicarious thrill of seeing violence done or sexuality enacted but refuse us an analytical framework by which to understand what is happening. Cain is deliberately declining the paradigms of explication upon which so much other detective fiction rests.

Maynard's thesis that the rise of detective fiction in the nineteenth century was concurrent with the development of bourgeois rationalism needs to be examined in this light. The impact of the Depression years produced, it seems to me, a diminished belief in the capacity of the individual and rational mind to comprehend, make sense of, and engage with the economic and social disaster that descended on the United States in 1929. Alongside this was the rising popularity of Freud's thinking during this period. This double assault on the idea that the individual consciousness can rationally explain the world beyond itself or, indeed, even itself is crucial to Cain. He has no interest in unravelling the unexplained through an analytical process. Rather, he presents violence in the context of sexuality and the quest for money. These are the causes of his narrators' activities, but they do not act, as such, as clues to their behaviour. Character development, in itself, plays no part in furthering the narrative.

What does generate the forward motion of the narrative is Cain's much-remarked rapid development of plot; his ability to 'jolt' the reader on every page – a process facilitated by his style. By refusing access to the internal mechanisms of the protagonist's mind, our attention is focused onto events. The first chapter of *The Postman Always Rings Twice* is a prime example of this technique. In approximately 700 words, of which over a third are devoted to directed or reported speech, we are presented in almost cinematic fashion with all of the essential information out which the complete narrative will be made over the remaining seventy-nine pages. Two notable and significant absences in this opening chapter are, first, any mention of Cora's name and, secondly, any insight into the motivations of Nick (who simply 'wanted something') or Frank: 'her lips stuck out in a way that made me want to mash them in for her'. By focusing on external details, and limiting self-understanding to its most basic level, Cain creates a world in which opaque characters move and respond.

The model being established, then, is not one of causality but one of juxtaposition. As readers we are granted a privileged position from which we recognise and understand motivation in a fashion unavailable to the characters themselves. A gap is opened between our understanding of the characters and the pattern of comprehension taking place in the text, a gap which is usually filled by the absent investigative narrator. As readers, we are not being invited to read an analysis of events passed, which explains these events through re-creation, but to see the events as they happened. Juxtaposition within the telling of these events allows condensation to take place and produces figures beyond the narrator who manifest the gamut of his contradictory impulses. This condensation is controlled by narrative, producing figures whose composite nature is revealed as the story moves forward. And, given the earlier description of the association between sexuality, violence, and destruction, this motion propels the narrator towards a position beyond his control and understanding. His capacity to influence the world he inhabits is stripped away until he becomes little more than a cork tossed back and forth by psychological and physical forces greater than himself.

This basic pattern is repeated in *The Postman Always Rings Twice* and *Double Indemnity*, as the female characters move from external description through a sudden sexual encounter towards an assertion which jams sexuality and violence together. It would be a mistake, though, to see *Double Indemnity* as a simple repetition of the earlier – and instantly successful – mode because, whereas *The Postman Always Rings Twice* remains locked firmly within the environment of Depression California, *Double Indemnity* breaks out into a world of nightmare: a world which resonates with Coleridge and Poe. This movement was, clearly, seen as a weakness by Chandler in his screen adaptation of the novel, removing it as it does from the familiar resources of the *film noir*.[11] But as an advance in 'the art of letting a story secrete its own adrenalin' it is clearly a step forward, for it tears Walter loose from the world of calculation and plunges him headlong into the almost furious space of his released desires and fears. Keyes, by allowing Walter to go free, unlocks a door into a more terrible punishment: a pact with the female figure of death. Walter's writing fragments as the last few connections with the world he understands break down.

But, for this process to work successfully, the text must move from the world of the realities of thirties California into the near (or complete) Gothic, which is the narrative equivalent to the psychological plunge into horror. When the novels begin in an environment in the slightest way exotic – by which I mean anything beyond the California Cain knew so well – they fail. Equally well, when they remain at the level of thirties California they are weakened by this lack of movement. The radical transformation worked on *Mildred Pierce* by Hollywood is an indication that Cain's contemporaries recognised this. The tale of Mildred's movement through the world of business remains determinedly suburban in the original, whilst Kady's sexual desires in *The Butterfly* are simply (in Cain's terms) perverse. Without the establishment of 'normality' and 'abnormality' as correlatives to each other, the books do not exploit Cain's capacity to move beyond a more or less interesting (but simple) social critique into some sort of 'native American expressionism', or to set slightly tired elements of the Gothic within a functioning social environment.

Cain's persistent return to the confessional model in his fiction indicates not so much a failure of imagination as a recognition of the proximity between the commission of a crime and the need to tell of it. In this, he stands in a line which begins not with Christie's *The Murder of Roger Ackroyd* (where the revelation that the author is the murderer is used simply as an ingenious trick), but with Coleridge and Poe's understanding of the ways in which guilt can inspire the telling of a tale. His past tense is not the past historic of other crime novelists, within which events are enclosed; it is a tense in which the past is lived out in the present act of writing.

Notes

1. W. M. Frohock, *The Novel of Violence in America* (Dallas: Southern Methodist University Press, 1957) p. 13.
2. Alain Robbe-Grillet, *'Snapshots' and 'Towards a New Novel'* (London: Caldar and Boyars, 1965) p. 72.
3. James M. Cain, *The Five Great Novels* (London: Picador 1985) p. 558.
4. Ibid., p. 236.
5. Ibid., p. 235.
6. Ibid., p. 559.
7. Ibid., p. 203.
8. *The Selected Letters of Raymond Chandler*, ed. Frank MacShane (London: Cape, 1981) p. 23.
9. Cain, *The Five Great Novels*, p. 323.
10. Ibid., p. 84.
11. Chandler did write draft versions of equivalent scenes for the film, but they were abandoned at an early stage.

8

Towards a Semiotic Reading of Mickey Spillane

ODETTE L'HENRY EVANS

Crime fiction is often seen as ephemeral, the reading being valid only in so far as excitement and suspense are created by the difficulty of finding out who is the perpetrator of the murder, or murders, recounted there; once he has been unmasked, it seems that the book can legitimately be discarded.

Roland Barthes, however, argues against this attitude, typical, he says, of a modern consumer society, and offers as an alternative the text seen as 'plural'[1] – that is to say, considered in such a way that there is no first reading different from all subsequent ones. This text, taken as a 'signifier', may furnish a multiplicity of meanings – provided that one reads and rereads it 'freely' without being held back by any traditional cultural constraints.

This is what a semiotic approach facilitates, since it makes it possible, in the well-known formula of McLuhan, to see the medium as the message, and to go beyond themes and meaning, in order to understand its systems and codes. Moreover, it enhances the appreciation of the text, as it reveals clearly its overall structural itinerary, and underlines the rich variety of functions available for the reader's scrutiny.

Crime fiction is obviously particularly well suited to this, since, by its very nature, it calls for a rigorously organised narrative structure, with no unexplained loose ends, making it a perfectly 'bounded' text.[2] An added interest is that such a strict sequential pattern makes it possible and indeed very rewarding to work at multitextual level, and to consider together several novels – here the novels of Mickey Spillane[3] (just as it makes it possible to consider variants of a same text simultaneously, as Propp did with his Russian fairy tale).

Considered in that light, the itinerary of Spillane's crime fiction becomes readily identifiable, in a way that can be expressed as

$$(S_1 \cup S_2) \dashrightarrow (S_1 \cap S_2)$$

where Subject 1, or S_1, is the hero, and S_2 the villain.

Little biographical information is available regarding Mickey Spillane himself, variously listed in the British Library as Frank Harrison Spillane and Frank Morrison Spillane. From the dedications of his books, one learns of the existence of a wife, and also that he was in the US Air Force during the war, probably fighting against the Japanese. His best-known characters are Mike Hammer, a private detective, and Tiger Mann, a secret agent; there are a few others, such as Phil Rocca, or Cat Fallon, the flier, but they all share the same characteristics, and act in much the same way, making it possible to consider them, for the present purpose, as the 'hero'.

In every novel there is of course a plot, expressed in natural language: that is to say – to use the Saussurean terminology – that there is a combination of the signified (the story that it tells) and of the signifier (the linguistic form). No literary criticism is intended here, and only the latter will be considered, the signified being used purely to provide relevant illustrations.

In essence, detective stories are a developing search, a *quest* for the identification of the villain, usually a killer (S_2), conducted by the investigator, the hero (S_1) who may, but need not, be a professional detective. S_1, whatever the plot, will display the permanent features of courage, integrity, acumen, while S_2 will add cruelty, callousness, and duplicity to the slyness needed to remain undetected and appear just as one of the outsiders.

From this, the whole narrative schema can be determined and its different perspectives identified. An initial sequence must introduce the hero – a hero who, in the novels of Mickey Spillane, is also the narrator, so that the subject of the discourse is also the subject of its enunciation. This renders virtually impossible a qualificative perspective where the qualities of S_1 could be explicitly described. Yet there are a few instances of this, when the hero, taking stock, reflects upon himself and his place in the scheme of things:

I lived to kill so that others could live. I lived to kill because my soul was a hardened thing that revelled in the thought of taking the blood of the bastards who make murder their business – I

was the evil that opposed other evil, leaving the good and the
meek in the middle to live and inherit the earth.

(*One Lonely Night*, p. 51[4])

Such moments of introspection are rare, and more complete
descriptions rely on the narrative perspective, using a process of
acquisitions, such as other characters' attitude or comments which
highlight the hero's qualities.

His physical charisma is emphasised in every novel, and he is
unfailingly attractive to women, from the bobby-soxer in *The Snake*
to the elderly theatrical dresser in *I, The Jury*, from the celebrated
Olympic athlete in *Bloody Sunrise* to the gangster's daughter in *The
Seven Year Kill*, to say nothing of the faithful secretary Velda of the
Hammer series.

His courage is shown either by the fear he inspires – 'I put the 32
up against his neck.... He handed over [his] 45 real easy, licking
his lips and trying to say something. The one beside me said:
"Look, Mac..."' (*The Snake*, p. 56); or by his reputation – 'You
aren't only on the "A" list [assassination list] over there now.
You're the top name. An assigned target' (*Bloody Sunrise*, p. 87).
Similarly, the hero's integrity is made clear throughout, in narrative form – nowhere better than in the closing episode of *The Snake*,
when Mike Hammer walks away without a backward glance at the
bank bags containing $3 million. Intellectual perception is an even
more essential ingredient if the hero is to succeed in his quest, and
Spillane's heroes are no exception. An interesting fact is that they
all work side by side with the police force, which they invariably
respect and trust. Mike Hammer's best friend, for instance, is the
young cop Pat Travers, and Hammer will immediately tell him
what he has discovered, often ending his tale with 'Now you got
everything I know.' Pat Travers, however, is not slow in acknow-
ledging Hammer's outstanding mental penetration:

> Great! Facts are one thing but there's still that crazy mind of
> yours. You make the same facts come out different answers
> somehow.... Oh, I agree, you're cooperative and all that jazz.
> You lay it on the line like you are requested to do.... But all the
> time you're following a strange line of reasoning nobody who
> looks at the facts would take. (*The Snake*, p. 104)

The fact can therefore be established that the status of S_1, while explicated by himself only in a very limited way, in what Greimas terms the reflexive doing (*faire-réfléchir*),[5] appears more usually through the intervention of the other characters, by transitive doing (*faire-transitif*).

The narrative pattern, or trajectory, develops further the 'doing' form of discourse, and a distinction can be drawn between pragmative and cognitive doing. Here, though, as no textual analysis will be attempted, only the cognitive doing will require investigation.

This cognition element lends itself to subdivision into further elements, the narrative and the communicative (both in relation to syntax), each of these being in turn open to as many secondary subdivisions as needed, once the transitional axis has been established.

Denominations, which correlate the definitions, form an important component of the discourse. Immediately evident, for instance, is the anthroponymy of the surname 'Hammer'. The denomination has a definite semantic content which, at the lexamatic level, increases the disjunction murderer–avenger.

Hammer, as a substantive, can be related to the tool, relentlessly flattening, driving into the ground, getting rid of the obstacle, striking the nail, in a way that leads on to the metaphorical notion of 'hitting the nail on the head'. A hammer can also be a weapon, and in that sense able to deliver crippling blows, to crush, to smash – thus introducing the notion of ruthlessness; it can relate to a gun, being the metal block which explodes the charge – not surprising, perhaps, since the hero 'packs a 32'. One way or another, all Spillane heroes have guns and use them.

Without indulging in a similar semantic exercise with other names, its relevance is equally evident for Tiger Mann (his real name, he states in *Bloody Sunrise*, given to him by his father), which nevertheless leads the beautiful Russian defector to call out to him with gratitude 'My Tiger!' in her quaintly accented English. Another such name is Cat Fallon, certainly a man of feline charm and cunning, under the rugged exterior of a former Air Force pilot making a living in a small airport in the fifties, having bought obsolete war 'planes cheaply.

I sat there with the half finished coffee in my hand, watching them service the battered old Mustang on the runway outside. There was nothing of interest there. But the blonde, reflected in the plate-glass window, was interesting especially when she knew I was watching, and arranged so I could see her legs from the best angle.... She was a dream.... Her hair ... like a Summer sunset.... The trouble was, I knew her, only she did not know me. Three years ago, she had interviewed me in a German hospital.... My face was bandaged and hurt from a shrapnel slice. That time, she had played the part in a nurse's outfit. (*The Flier*, p. 9)

As one can see, he will be like the cat playing with a mouse.

In *The Erection Set*, a later and much longer book, published in 1972, the hero is called Dogeron Kelly – an old Irish name, admittedly, but one that will inevitably be shortened to 'Dog Kelly', or simply 'Dog'. Here again, he is not a professional detective or secret agent, but a former Army man, a devoted and stubborn individual who had now come back to avenge his mother's misery and claim his inheritance. 'The same old, damn, disreputable Dog is here!' (*The Erection Set*, p. 11).

Then, considering the hero himself as *actant* (the proper semiotic term for 'character', as one who acts, or is acted upon), he becomes more and more effective and powerful as knowledge is acquired – in a way, like little Tom Thumb of the fairy tale – while the villain remains what he is from the start: one could say, pursuing further the comparison with fairy-tale characters, like the ogre, big and bad from time immemorial.

Narrative perspectives explicate the acquisition of the necessary competence by the hero, competence which replaces progressively the initial *lack*, to borrow a Proppian definition, and is what allows the plot to move forward.

In addition, at the semantic level, there is a constant system of exchange of opposites – dominant versus dominated – which represents the second of the three stages of discourse commonly referred to as *confrontation – domination – consequence*. It is at that intermediate stage that are situated the instances of success of the hero S_1 against the villain S_2, and this applies to Spillane's characters. Indeed, the sequential division of his novels is on the whole striking. It is possible to pinpoint accurately any occurrence demonstrating a form of dominance leading to eventual submission of the opponent. In other words, the *exchange* situated on the sender–receiver axis lends itself to identification throughout.

The most striking example is perhaps the novel already mentioned, *Bloody Sunrise*, presented as a sequence of four sunrises. The first sunrise (confrontation) heralds the day when, in the first lines of the novel, Tiger Mann resigns from the secret service in order to get married, entering a new life of peace and happiness, free from constraints or danger. However, a 'phone call interferes with this: 'Tiger, you are on an assignment. Plato. Plato was the big one. Kill or be killed. The entire structure of America was in trouble. The alternate answer was war' (*Bloody Sunrise*, p. 15). This sudden deprivation of freedom is the negative element which will lead Tiger Mann to pit his wits against Russian intelligence.

The second sunrise is the dawn meeting of Tiger and the Russian defector Sonia Dutko. She is beautiful, attracts him and they make love. Here, the axis reference (within the discourse) is in fact the conjunction of the subject S_1 with the object of the quest – even though the latter is still unidentified, in accordance with the required 'quality' of S_2, which is the ability to deceive.

> It was a beautiful sunrise, slow and easy at first, then with crashing suddenness, the wild red and bright burst in upon us both in a frenzy of delight, then diminished into the steadily increasing glow of morning.   (p. 73)

In addition, the subcode as symbolism of love-making is easily identifiable here.

The third sunrise mentioned in the novel comes after a terrible night of ambush and killing, which has left two dead, but, when Tiger has been able to prevent Sonia from being captured by 'phony' US Treasury men, a deed which leads her to trust him sufficiently to ask him to save another Russian defector.

> She touched my arm lightly, the pressure of her fingers pleading: 'You will do something then?'
> 'Something.'
> Above us the sky split with the suddenness of all storms coming to an end and the pale ruby glow of a sunrise came through to warm the night.   (p. 111)

The movement of the discourse is twofold, with two inverse narrative programmes, recognisable although S_2 is still unidentified. The acquisition of power – taking the initiative for further action – balances the increasing helplessness of Sonia, demonstrated by her actual begging.

Thus, the second and third sunrises clearly belong to the median stage of progressive *domination*.

The last sunrise, and indeed the final paragraph of the novel will elicit the *consequence*, and decisively suppress the opposition between S_1 and S_2 in what is the third stage of the discourse trajectory. This is the definitive dispossession or deprivation of the villain S_2, through a subject of doing (*faire*) other than himself. In the transitive disjunction, it is in fact Sonia, the Russian 'defector', who dies, following the final unravelling of the plot.

> The sun was just coming up in the east, the crescent tip of a brilliant orange, reaching out to light the earth with fiery fingertips of a new day. Sonia was still there with me, but she wasn't watching the sunrise. In essence, she was almost a part of it, a sparkling wet, red splash on the gray rubble of the building that reflected the glow of a fresh day and a job that was all over.
>
> (p. 159)

The reversal is complete. Sonia has been unmasked as the real Soviet agent, not only endangering the life of Tiger and other American agents, but also trying to prevent the genuine defector from speaking to the free world, thus defusing the situation and preventing a war breaking out. Sonia was blown up when the whole building exploded. Assignment Plato has been completed, and Tiger Mann's freedom is renewed.

The text is established as turning on a thematic axis, moving between two exclusive positions:

vice	←-- | --→	virtue
power	←-- | --→	helplessness
love	←-- | --→	hate

As the semic axis is a positive versus a negative opposition, the originally recognised opposition which initiates the novel's trajectory finds itself submerged through a linking-together (concatenation) of surmises, and of events, leading eventually to an evidence of duplicity and – inevitably – of swift retribution.

This makes it possible to establish the corresponding semiotic square:

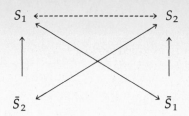

←-----→ contrary (the presence of the one presupposes the presence of the other)

←——→ contradictory

——— complementary

S_1---S_2 axis of opposites

$\bar{S}_1$---$\bar{S}_2$ axis of sub-opposites

$\bar{S}_1$---$\bar{S}_2$ ⎫ deixic axes (positive
$\bar{S}_1$---S_2 ⎬ and negative)

Then, having considered the semantic investment of the hero S_1 with the villain S_2, the final doing (*faire*), the unmasking, can be examined. This involves a double transformation, where each subject becomes at the same time an object for the other, which can be shown as

$$(S_1 \cup OS_2) \;\dashrightarrow\; (S_1 \cap OS_2)$$
$$(S_2 \cup OS_1) \;\dashrightarrow\;)S_2 \cap OS_1)$$

where S_1 is the hero, while OS_2 is the villain as *object* of the quest. S_1's initiative, resulting from his intellectual powers of deduction, is simultaneous with the disjunction corresponding to the dispossession of S_2.

Such intellectual perspicacity can occur in different ways. It can be slow, advancing by degrees towards the final unmasking:

It took a long time to get around to it, but I did. Funny, the way things worked out. All the symptoms were backwards. I had the wrong ones figured for it until the slip came. They all make that one slip.... (*I, The Jury*, p. 149)

Discovery of the truth can in fact be almost too late for the hero:

The metallic click of the hammer of a gun coming back was louder than all the other sounds, it was like a crashing cymbal stroke next to my ear.

> The guy said: 'I'll put him in cold storage, good, Mannie.'
> Too late the warmth of knowledge reached me. Too late did I
> finally understand the reasoning of a woman, untrained in the
> devious. . . .
>   I could feel myself trying to withdraw from what was coming,
> my brain pleading for a numbed body to move, to hide. . . .
>   There were more rolling thunders and loud voices. . . . Hands
> went under me, sat me up, and a voice . . . said: 'Phil! Phil! You
> all right?'   (*The Seven Year Kill*, p. 167)

The police were there, fortunately, and had shot the hired killer
just in time to let the hero free to complete the task.

Usually, the hero's mind works somewhat faster. As for the
reader, this varies with each individual, although the clues are
there for him to work on as well. This question of clues focuses the
attention on the functions of each message. These will be placed
between the initial and final sequences: that is to say, if the
trajectory of the discourse is seen as linear, in the centre section (in
other words, in the median actualisation of the discourse).

In order to constitute a clue, a message must have several
functions, not all of them initially perceivable. If one refers back,
for example, to the meeting of Tiger with the Russian girl, when
they make love, one would perhaps not be aware that this is one of
the rare instances of sexual intercourse in a Spillane novel, and
undoubtedly the only one actually described. Usually the hero is in
love, but does not allow his feelings to get the better of him; all is
subordinated to the task that he has set himself.

However, one is here witnessing a detailed episode. Sonia's
clothes are soaked through, and in the house where she had been
offered asylum, the house of Tiger Mann's fiancée, she has found a
lovely white negligée which she has put on, over her own
underwear:

> Beneath the white was the dark outline of the briefest under-
> clothes with a strange raised pattern that had an exciting, exotic
> effect, a skimpy bra that barely covered the crest of her breasts
> and left a wide, wide expanse of pink skin.
>   (*Bloody Sunrise*, p. 107)

There is a referential function here: we know what Sonia is
wearing. There is also an emotive function: it is sexually attractive.

There is, in addition, a phatic function, or perhaps, more accurately, a phatic intent: we feel that this underwear is somewhat lacking in good taste, in 'class' so to speak, that it is not what a demure young woman would be wearing. Indeed, an explanation is provided for this. Sonia blushes and explains that, in Russia, women have no opportunity to wear anything frilly and feminine; it is too 'capitalistic' – an explanation which seems satisfactory in the circumstances.

However, later we find Tiger raiding a block of offices, following a lead. In a small room, a mail-order business is conducted which yields nothing significant besides the other suspicious possibilities: a bookmaker without a telephone, a film-processing studio with 'blue movies'. The mail-order room only had catalogues of household gadgets, gimmicks, bikinis, stockings, bought wholesale and sent by post to listed customers.

Tiger will eventually realise the truth, and he will act swiftly. He will then rejoin Sonia and confront her with her treachery:

> 'Your group is gone, Sonia. We busted your communications and you are wide open.' She turned to me. She had to be sure. . . . 'How?'
> I said: 'Your pretty little exotic bikini underwear, chicken. It gave you away. Your communications with Fountain [the mail-order firm] were always covered [with] order blanks. With the return instructions, he sent you items of merchandise. Oh, nothing special, nothing any dame with taste would wear. . . . Your taste was lousy and you couldn't bring yourself to toss the stuff away. When I saw the junk Fountain had stored away, I should have known then . . .'   (*Bloody Sunrise*, p. 154)

– which, of course, explains the last sunrise, when she is killed in the explosion. Also noticeable is the fact that each successive sunset is redder than the last, representing another phatic intent.

The transitive disjunction further brings to light some subprogrammes of narrative which relate to different modalities – those, for instance, of knowledge, duty, ability and desire. Ability (*pouvoir*) is part of the essential make up of the hero, as is his sense of duty (*devoir*); his knowledge (*savoir*) is expressed through the various clues or functions of the message, but his desire (*vouloir*), which will be different according to the story, can already be part of the hero's chosen profession as detective, or secret agent. It can also be something personal:

> Jack [the murdered man] was about the best friend I ever had. . . . I am not letting the killer go through the tedious process of the law. . . . The dead can't speak for themselves. . . . Nobody in the [jury] box would know how it felt to be dying. . . . The law is fine, but this time, I'm the law and I'm not going to be cold and impartial. . . .   (*I, The Jury*, p. 9)

Considering further that modality of desire, it is important to explore the possibility of a mediating influence of S_2 which could affect partially the general syntactic transformation – if, for instance, the villain were to invite, through some kind of subconscious causality, the subsequent action of S_1. Such desire would be seen not in the psychological field, but in the semiotic modality of wanting, the behaviour of the villain 'attracting the wrath' of the hero and arousing his desire for revenge.

In that sense, the event itself, the murder and its circumstances, provides the necessary information. The relation between S_1 and S_2 must then be considered in the optic of this initial object of the event, the murder, which can conveniently be represented as $O[m]$.

Normally, one can expect the encounter of S_1 with $O[m]$ at the beginning of the novel, and indeed initiating the action. Mickey Spillane himself comments, 'You can always make a perfect start with a dead man. It's an ultimate end and a perfect beginning' (*The Snake*, p. 35). A death need not, however, be an obvious homicide, and the encounter of S_1 with $O[m]$ only as a presumed natural death precludes investigation until later in the narrative. Thus, in *The Flier*, there is nothing strange, at first sight, in the fact that the old 'buddy' of an ex-Air Force pilot left him in his will the small airport he had set up. It is only later that it will seem possible, then likely, and finally evident, that the death of the 'buddy' as a result of a 'plane crash had been anything but an accident.

More complex is the encounter of S_2 with $O[m]$, in so far as the nature of a murder requires it to be hidden, and the spatial conjunction will be that of successive axes, the most simple being

(a) S_1 unknowing/S_2 undetected (b) S_1 suspicious/S_2 suspected
(c) S_1 knowing   /S_2 identified (d) S_1 acting   /S_2 unmasked

This can also assume a more complex pattern, such as

(a) S_1 unknowing/S_2 undetected   (b) S_1 setting / S_2 trying to
                                            himself as / destroy S_1
                                            bait

'When does the fox outfox the fox?' (*The Erection Set*, p. 311).
   A possible variation of the second pattern is identified at times:

(b) S_1 setting up / S_2 walking into the trap
      a trap   / and unmasking himself

'I slid down into the lushness of the cushions to make myself comfortable, then pulled the 45 from its holster and snapped the safety off. I waited for the killer' (*I, The Jury*, p. 151).
   If one takes the transformation to be T, one can plot the initial disjunction to the final state in that way:

$$T\,[S_1 \dashrightarrow (S_2 \cup O[m])\,]$$

into

$$T\,[S_1 \dashrightarrow (S_2 \cap O[m])\,]$$

This transformation may be effected in a variety of ways. It can take the form of an exchange, where the killer volunteers some information to secure the trust of S_1. Such a modality of exchange can be discerned in the following conversation:

   'Well, you look like a cop, but cops aren't interested in me any more.'
   When I did not answer, he chuckled. 'I have had lots of experience with cops. What do you want to know?'
   'You own this place?'
   'Yes, thirty years, saving a few cents a day, but that is not what you want to know.'
   I laughed and nodded. 'Okay, Sonny, it's about a promise you made long ago to kill Sim Torrence.'
   'Yeah, I get asked that lots of times.... Guess I was pretty mad, back then.' He smiled patiently and pushed his glasses up.... 'I'm old. I think different. I don't have those old

feelings.... I just don't care.... Sounds silly?'
  'Not so silly, Sonny.'
  He coughed.... 'Ah, yeah, they were the days, but the fire is
out now.'   (*The Snake*, p. 62)

Sonny is in fact Sim Torrence's killer, as will be revealed later,
when his skilful display of benign old age and trustworthiness is
exposed: 'His face had lost the tired look and his eyes were
bright.... There was nothing stooped about him now, nothing of
the old man there' (p. 154). Fortunately for society, his act will not
go unpunished.

At other times, the modality is one of gift, where witnesses come
forward, for example, despite personal risks, because they are
concerned that justice should be done. More usual, however, is the
modality of discovery, made through powers of observation or of
deduction, on the part of S_1.

With the appreciation of these sub-programmes of narration and
of their various modalities, it is possible to map out accurately the
discursive trajectory of the novels, and indeed to establish what
makes crime-fiction writings different from other literary forms. A
suitable semiotic square can be created, expressing the four main
terms: *truth* (what is fact), *lie* (what is pretence), *secret* (what is
hidden) and *falsity* (what is not true).

Considering the axes of opposites in the semiotic square, one can
define

being $[e]$
appearing $[p]$
non-being $[\bar{e}]$
non-appearing $[\bar{p}]$

where these actantial roles can be related to the thematic role. For
the hero S_1,

e corresponds to his status as private detective, secret agent,
  avenger
$\bar{e}$ corresponds to his situation, condition
p corresponds to his intuition, mental ability
$\bar{p}$ corresponds to his initial ignorance of the truth

Four terms can be identified, which can be represented by A, B, C and D on the semiotic square:

$A = e + p$ which is fact (truth)
$B = \bar{e} + p$ which is not true (lie)
$C = e + \bar{p}$ which is hidden (secret)
$D = \bar{e} + \bar{p}$ which is pretence (falseness)

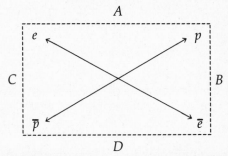

In the initial sequence, the hero is in D $(= \bar{e} + \bar{p})$. The first transformation will lead from $\bar{p}$ to p, from his non-being to appearing, $\bar{e} + p$, position B, which is a false one, because of the trickery of the villain under his particular disguise. The hero, still unknowing, accepts what the villain pretends to be, but as his ability exerts itself, $\bar{e}\text{---}e$, he moves to A, which for S_1 is the position of truth $(e + p)$.

The second sequence is articulated around the spatial disjunction where, first, the unexpected action of S_2, in his disguised secret position, brings S_1 to unravel at least part of the truth $(e + \bar{p})$ – in other words, what is but does not then appear to be – while S_2 moves from p to $\bar{p}$, bringing him away from B to D. Simultaneously, $p \text{ ---> } \bar{p}$ for S_1 causes him to move from A to C (his secret). Then comes the second interpretative doing $e \text{ ---> } \bar{e}$ where the full understanding of the situation, the unmasking, brings S_1 back to D. What S_1 had thought to be true $(A = e + p)$ is eventually revealed as false, while what seemed false $(\bar{e} + \bar{p})$ turns out to be the truth. The opposite, of course, applies to S_2.

It is therefore clear that the moment of unmasking is the essential point of the discursive trajectory, as evidenced by its two different and opposite functions. It is as Spillane describes it: 'The quick excitement of life and the feeling of accomplishment. The spicy competition that was in reality a constant war of nerves with all the intrigue and action of actual conflict' (*The Seven Year Kill*, p. 92).

It is relatively easy to reach this central point, since, as Spillane also explains, there are only a limited number of reasons for committing a murder: 'First classify all murders: There are only a few. War – Passion – Self-protection – Insanity – Profit and Mercy' (*I, The Jury*, p. 27).

In the final instance, the comparison made between the hero and Tom Thumb, who learnt as he went, and between the villain and the ogre, man-eater from birth, is verified, in so far as the square demonstrates that S_2 has not changed fundamentally, but that S_1 has progressed through every intermediary sequence, acquiring desire (*vouloir*) and knowledge (*savoir*) leading to the ability (*faire*) to exact retribution from S_2.

As the text appears in its fullness, the heroic actants, Mike Hammer, Tiger Mann, Cat Fallon and others, are defined according to their semiotic function, in relation to their direct opposites, the villains, until the latter's final unmasking and retribution.

The purpose of undertaking the semiotic study of a text, and of establishing its semiotic square, is to make the rereading of that text (in the present instance, a series of novels) identical to the first reading, just as it places that initial reading on a par with any subsequent reading, as it were. Each time, the text is re-created in its plurality, the same and yet always new.

Notes

1. R. Barthes, *S/Z* (Paris: Seuil, 1977).
2. J. Kristeva, 'The Bounded Text', tr. T. Gora, in *Desire in Language* (Oxford: Blackwell, 1980) pp. 36–63.
3. Spillane's children's story *The Day the Sea Rolled Back* (London: Methuen, 1981) is omitted from the present study.
4. Quotations from Mickey Spillane's novels are from the Corgi Transworld editions, published in London: *Bloody Sunrise* (1966), *The Erection Set* (1972), *The Flier* (1964), *I, The Jury* (1960), *One Lonely Night* (1951), *The Seven Year Kill* (1964), *The Snake* (1965). Page references are given in the text.
5. French terms are included to provide cross-referencing with A. J. Greimas, *Sémiotique. Dictionnaire raisonné de la théorie du langage* (Paris: Hachette, 1979), which is still the most authoritative work on the subject.

9

Very Nearly GBH: Savouring the Texts of George V. Higgins

MICHAEL J. HAYES

With just the minimum of phonological fuss we can turn GBH into GVH: Grievous Bodily Harm becomes George V. Higgins. The transformation is so easily achieved by merely turning the plosive bi-labial *b* into a lip-biting labio-dental *v*. To continue the image, the blustering explosion of physical violence, which has Bernie Morgan 'Beatin' the shit out of' the kid who scratches his car is succeeded by the shrewd pragmatism of the likes of Lyle Putter, who will 'bite [his] lower lips if necessary clean through [to] cut a fucking deal with Bernie Morgan'.[1]

The artful game with the initial letters could be expanded thematically to produce a view of the novels as exploring the conflict between violence and cunning in the lower depths. That tale would be as specious as the phonological sleight of hand that started it running. Readers of this essay have perhaps willingly colluded with me so far, maybe even mouthing a silent *b* to *v*, or at least recognising the mimetic possibilities suggested by the game. But for the vast majority of readers the reality is what Derrida says it is: the written sounds are fatherless and, like the written words, orphans. On the page the letters are without an articulating parent; with no speaker present the words stand in isolation from a sentient origin which would root them in a present context, an actuality. On the page words are all too easily shadows of shadows, as Joyce and Derrida have demonstrated: 'words' can slip to 'weird' or to 'ward', its ambivalent presence a key to uncertainties. The word may be weird in its texture of haunting relationships, wounding us, as Hartman suggests,[2] by its fickleness, its awful openness to interpretation. Or the same word can be a talisman to ward off evil, a healing presence bestowing a benediction.

115

If readers play the game, agreeing some significance to the move from *b* to *v*, then Higgins's novels might for example be discussed in terms of the psychological portrayal of criminal types or the social determinants of criminality. Questions such as 'How real is Eddie Coyle?' and 'Is it plausible that he should end up in a '68 Ford Galaxie with nine .22s in his skull?' could be tested against what we know of such characters both from fact and fiction. Alternatively we can match what we learn about low life in Boston with police reports, probation reports and journalistic 'true crime' features which write of such events and characters with the intention of giving an authentic picture.

Reviewers of the books, who at present dominate the list of contributory writings, have from the start focused on the notion of a hard-edged authenticity. In particular they have emphasised the veracity of the dialogue: 'Authentic as the crack of a .38'; 'a true ear for the spoken word'; 'Higgins writes some of the best going, dialogue with pit-of-the-stomach laughs or a cold gasp of dawning implications.'[3] This emphasis on the dialogue is understandable, since the books, particularly the crime fiction, are predominantly written in dialogue form. Of the early novels, for example, *The Friends of Eddie Coyle* and *Cogan's Trade* are approximately 85 per cent dialogue, with 2–3 per cent more made up of phrases that entail the function 'he said'. Even by the standards of popular fiction, which are often three-quarters dialogue, this proportion is very high. But to claim that the language is authentic in the 'tape-recorder true' style is as contrived an agreement between text and reader as that which was called into play at the beginning of this essay.

The dialogue Higgins writes has features which deviate from what we are accustomed to in written dialogue. These features, semantic and syntactic, are purposely written in to signal to the reader 'these are badges of authenticity'. Taking a few syntactic examples from *The Digger's Game*,[4] we see that the commonest form is to disrupt our expectations of what is likely to come next; the normal pattern of structure is broken.

You, I think you're gonna have to find something a lot bigger'n radios to sell, you expect to make that kind of dough.   (p. 15)

... to get half a bath in the, where the pantry was, ...

(p. 19)

Less frequently Higgins experiments with the omission of prepositions, as in 'and you go the bank' (p. 16).

Characteristic as these incompleted structures might be of real talk, they are, in the books, no more than a few representatives of what happens in speech. (Moreover, as his books have gained a wider readership, so Higgins seems to have used them more sparingly, even possibly as indexes to individual characters something after the fashion of Dickens.) What these devices do is not merely to remind us of real talk or that the origin of the reading game is life itself, but also to push us into a closer, more unsettled relationship with that initiating 'real life'.

The games we play in fictions relate to life in a variety of ways – there has been the easy assumption for many years that popular fictions offer pleasure and distraction by over-simplifying life, making its abrasive complexities palatably anodyne, heightening its joys and tragedies by the evasion of moral responsibility. Literature, on the other hand, has high status as the veritable glass-bead game of fictions which in its complexities challenges our certainties about life.

The essays in the present collection seek to challenge that easy assumption of difference by scrutinising popular fictions and subjecting them to critical techniques that except in isolated instances have been reserved for literature. In the Higgins books – the particular focus of attention in this essay – people rob banks, burn buildings, steal dogs and kill people in a way consonant with crime fiction, but in addition to this they challenge and explore our ways of being in a number of directions.

Rabinowitz writes, 'Every literary theoretician these days needs a governing metaphor about texts: text as mirror, text as body, text as system.'[5] The word game that opened this essay is the 'governing metaphor' for my critical stance and what it spells out is that language can be considered as behaviour. As such, language resides on a continuum with what we normally class as behaviour – namely, non-language actions. At the extremes of the continuum are, respectively, language and action, but in the uncertain middle area we have language and action jostling each other for definition:

language	←—————————————————→	action
'Will this bank do?'	'What are you waiting for?' (pointing gun at teller)	Shoots bank teller

The purpose of the example is to demonstrate that language behaviour (speech acts) can be considered as entailing greater or lesser degrees of action (illocutionary force), just as the action, featuring as it does a 'teller', entails language-like communication. 'Will this bank do?', in the circumstances implied by our example, is a question primarily demanding a language response, but it can also be thought of as a directional gesture, a way of pointing to a specific place. When we come to the scene in the bank, the question 'What are you waiting for?', while having the same form as the earlier language, certainly does not demand a language response; though formed as a question it is really an exhortation, a command, a threat, and the first move, failing compliance, in the sentence of death whose full stop is the punctuating shot at the end.

That shot is also the signal that starts our inquiry proper on its way. We have an author, Higgins, whose books, even by the standards of popular fiction, contain a great deal of talk. They also belong to a genre noted for its hard, fast and violent action. Our point of reference, what is know in linguistics as speech-act theory, is that language can itself be seen as behaviour interacting to different degrees with other behaviours. The basic question I am asking is, does Higgins actively explore this complex relationship between language and action? The more sophisticated question is, if he does, so what?

The first question is harmless enough, and there would be no point in asking it if I were not already sure I could offer an answer. The second is much more troublesome, and I think I shall try to answer it with some encouragement from a Yale man, the critic Geoffrey Hartman. The sting is in place. But standing in the shadows is Higgins's professional killer, Cogan. If it all goes wrong the last words I'll hear are, 'The man says you've sold him short – to Literature. Well this is the last time you're gonna get to fuck with his corpus' – followed by four .38s from a Smith and Wesson Police Special.

Before *The Digger's Game* starts, Jerry Doherty, 'the Digger', is in debt to a Shylock for $18,000. As the owner of a working-men's bar the Digger does not have that kind of cash; he can neither buy up his markers nor pay off the weekly extortion. He has every reason to regret his three-day junket to Las Vegas, a trip organised by a dubious tour company that includes the equally dubious loan company. The trip was designed to let Las Vegas gambling relieve the tourists of their cash, and then more. In the Digger's case it was all too successful.

The narrative is the Digger's struggle to raise the money, any way he can – and he is not particularly fussy. But at the same time the 'junkets and sharking' company is undergoing some changes itself. The presiding genius, Mr Green, has recently managed to get a thirty-year sentence and there is pressure to go with the times and move the operation up-market. The protagonists face each other but they have each got their own problems.

In the tradition of crime fiction it is usually the pressure of violent actions, murder or robbery, that precipitates the narrative, or even in some instances is the narrative. In *Five Against the House* it is the meticulous planning to rob a particular and real-life casino which is the novel, while in Clive Eggleton's *Seven Days to a Killing* it is the kidnapping of a child which sets the story in motion. 'Like other realistic artists the good crime writer makes the familiar new. It is as if crime alone could make us see again, or imaginatively enough, to enter someone else's life.'[6]

In Higgins's books it is not crime which is the initiating force but pressure on the individual, and that pressure has only incidentally to do with crime. In *The Rat on Fire* pressure comes on one side in the shape of an ambitious newly appointed prosecutor, Terry Mooney, ranged against Jerry Fein, who, on the other side, is trying to get his apartment building back from its impoverished non-paying tenants. In *The Friends of Eddie Coyle* the real trouble is not the 200 cases of stolen Canadian Club that Eddie was caught transporting, but his family responsibilities and his sense of self: 'I got three kids and a wife at home, and I can't afford to do no more time, you know? The kids're growing up and they go to school and the other kids make fun of them and all. Hell, I'm almost forty-five years old.'[7] Even in what is probably Higgins's most orthodox crime book, *Cogan's Trade*, it is not fear which is the basis of Cogan's respect for Dillon: 'Nah, it wasn't that. It was, he knew the way things oughta be done, right?'[8]

There are two forces at work in the characters, their individual needs and their group membership. What is interesting is the tension between the two and the striving to come to some kind of acceptable accommodation. The stories are set in a very basic world where needs are simple; there is no final triumph for the individual, only the achievement of getting by for the present. 'The heroic rebel, warrior, or robber baron, earlier prototypes of successful competition, yield their place in the popular imagination to the wily veteran determined not so much to outstrip his opponents as to outlast them.'[9] All that most of Higgins's characters want to do is stay in the game – or, if they are a little higher in the hierarchy, as Cogan is, maybe just keep the game going. Their chief weapon is not the gun or baseball bat but language.

In 'Problems in Cetacean and other Mammalian Communication' Bateson suggests, 'What I am trying to say about wolves in particular, and about pre-verbal animals in general, is that their discourse is primarily about the rules and the contingencies of relationship.' Later in the essay, which is only marginally, but very provocatively, about human communication, he suggests that 'Our mammalian ancestry is very near the surface, despite recently acquired linguistic tricks.'[10] If we look for a while in some detail at *The Digger's Game* we see precisely that, that running through the book communication is about 'the rules and the contingencies of relationship'. In this context robbery, violence and murder are simply examples of communication at the desperate edge of discourse.

To return to the Digger: his problems, this time around anyway, started when he signed notes for $18,000 in Las Vegas. The book opens with two men in a car at night, the driver briefing 'the fat man' on burgling a nearby building. But much more is going on than a briefing: the driver and the fat man are engaged in an exchange that defines their relationship. Since we also learn that the fat man is the Digger, the exchange has in addition to introduce us to his character.

From the start the Digger resists any attempt at superiority or control on the part of the driver. 'What can I tell you, except be careful' is the kind of patronising exhortation superiors use to rally inferiors in a friendly way. The Digger's response is, 'Look, I'm gonna act like I was minding my own business' (p. 5), the implication being, 'and you mind yours'.

Next the driver wants the Digger to wear gloves. Again the Digger interprets this as an attempt to give him orders, an attempt he strongly resists. 'I don't like gloves', he says. In order to indicate the vigour, flexibility and subtlety of Higgins's dialogue we shall look at the next part of the exchange in some detail. (The letters and italics identify the main items of discourse discussed.)

'That's what I thought', the driver said, 'no gloves. I heard that about you. The Digger goes in *bare-ass.*'[a] The driver pulled a pair of black vinyl gloves out of the map pocket on his door. *'Wear these.'*[b]

The Digger took the gloves in his left hand. *'Whatever you say, my friend.*[c] It's your job.' *He put the gloves in his lap.*[d]

'No,' the driver said, *'I really mean it, Dig.*[e] You want to go in bare-ass, you go in bare-ass. That's all right with me. *But you get to that paper, the actual paper, you put them gloves on first,*[f] and you keep them on, *okay?'*[g]

'I wouldn't think it'd help then',[h] the Digger said. . . .

'Well, *take my word for it',*[i] the driver said, *'it does. It really does.*[j] . . . Now I really mean it, *you know?*[k] *This is for my protection.*[l] Gloves on as soon as you get to the paper.'

'Gloves on',[m] the Digger said.

The exchange is only partly about the gloves, much more it is the Digger's assertion of his independence, a cheeky but reckless defiance summed up in the expression 'to go in bare-ass'. On the driver's part it is a series of manoeuvres to contain the potentially dangerous recklessness of the Digger either by outright control or by persuasion.

(a)   The driver's use of 'bare-ass' may be considered a put-down, emphasising the boyish bravado of the Digger.

(b)   With 'Wear these', the driver resorts to an imperative, hoping to keep some control over the Digger.

(c)   The Digger apparently acquiesces with 'Whatever you say', but by adding of 'my friend' he emphasises the purely formal nature of his agreement. It means 'I heard what you said and I'll disarm your likely response to the spirit of my answer by calling you "friend".'

(d)   The verbal nature of the Digger's agreement is reinforced by 'It's your job', but the gesture of refusing to put on the gloves underlines his equivocal response to being ordered.

(e)   The driver picks up the evasion and insists, 'I really mean it', but the insistence is ameliorated by the use of companionable tag 'Dig'. Moreover, the earlier imperative is completely withdrawn as the driver concedes the Digger's right not to wear gloves if he does not want to.

(f)   The only stricture left is now at the practical level of getting the Digger to wear the gloves while actually stealing the paper.

(g) The driver has moved his position from trying to dominate the Digger to one of appealing for his co-operation. This appeal is reinforced by the question tag 'okay?' which invites the response 'sure, okay'.

(h) But the Digger still refuses to concede too readily to wearing the gloves or to the change in the discourse, in case either admission be seen as a sign of weakness. He does, however, accept the possibility of taking the tension out of the exchange by opting for the relatively neutral ground of observation: 'I wouldn't think it'd help then'.

(i) The driver gratefully accepts the Digger's shift, ingratiatingly laying himself on the line: 'take my word for it'.

(j) The new stance of the driver is emphasised by repeatedly assuring the Digger of the importance of his co-operation.

(k) Even when he repeats what he said earlier, under (e), instead of tagging it with a companionable 'Dig' he concedes even further and tags it with a question 'you know?' He is not for a moment asking the Digger to contradict him but formally conceding the possibility.

(l) Having given way to the Digger the driver now tries to build the relational side of the exchange. His statement 'This is for my protection' is a signal of his vulnerability, which he now acknowledges as the basis for his statement 'Gloves on'.

(m) Digger's response seals the new terms of the relationship, putting the gloves in their 'proper' perspective. When he echoes the driver's 'Gloves on' he is asserting his status in the relationship and affirming the wearing of the gloves as part of the mechanics of the robbery. It is interesting that even here he does not just say 'yes' but is careful to concede in terms equal to the driver.

Going back to the earlier point of my chosen prevailing metaphor, the words the two men use are part of the same communicating system as wearing the gloves. Presumably from the Digger's record the driver has reason to believe he will be difficult. To assert himself he enlists the gloves, which as a self-evidently necessary part of the basic plan he tries to extend into a means to dominate the Digger. The Digger resists the pressure but concedes the practicality of wearing the gloves, in so doing turning aside an attempt to dominate him instead making a practical concession, which puts the driver in his debt.

What is of further interest is that in winning his deal with the driver he establishes himself with the reader – it becomes the Digger and us not only against the world of the book but *against the author* as well. By calling the Digger 'The fat man, cramped in the passenger bucket', the author conspired with the driver to attempt to diminish him by making him a fat man with no name. His triumph over the driver in wringing the name 'Dig' out of him is also a triumph over an apparently reluctant author. The Digger is on the way to becoming one of those characters whose life exceeds the confines of the books for which they were created. The Digger's presence in the book is enunciated by his behaviour in the opening chapter. With the exception of the robbery in chapter 14, each of his appearances is the signal for an engagement of some kind, be it with his wife, brother, or the Greek who comes to collect the debt. Each of his linguistic encounters is a joust that takes place within a different part of his life.

With his wife he is unable to get the upper hand because he cannot get control of the discourse; at every turn she confronts him with the inescapable reality of their life together. To seal the argument about his weight, for example, she comments, 'You damned near crushed me, the last time' (p. 43). When he embarrasses her by reference to her sexuality she turns the conversation to the economics of everyday living, which of course culminates in a reference to the Las Vegas trip. She thinks it cost in all $1100 and that it 'is the worst thing you ever did, Jerry, the absolute worst thing' (p. 51).

Similarly, when he goes to Paul, his brother the priest, for help, his attempts to control the situation by controlling the conversation fail. His ploy is to refer to their family history, but at each initiative he is foiled by reality. When he tries to pressure Paul by pointing out that it was Paul who got all their mother's insurance money, facts reveal that it was actually Paul who was out of pocket, having met family expenses of which the Digger was unaware.

The Digger's failures to take control of the discourse with his wife and Paul mirror the limits within which he lives. With his wife the constraints are the everyday demands of providing for and nurturing a family, demands which to his credit he never denies though he does not always heed. With his brother the limits are set by the wider family context which has conditioned his life as we see it. The digger does not wangle money out of Paul; it is Paul who gives money to the Digger, and in doing so he has the power to demand promises of him: 'no more emergency visits, and no more crimes' (p. 77). The Digger promises because he has no option if he wants the $3000, but both he and we know that his promises are lies; the imperatives of gangland are too insistent.

But if the Digger has problems so have the people to whom he owes the money. Their collector is the Greek, an old-style hood; threats and violence, the late night 'phone call to the wife, the heavy mob, are the main ingredients of his vocabulary. Not only is his lexicon limited; he is also short on the ability to recognise what is going on. His very first appearance (p. 24) shows him pedantic, mean and unable to cope with life, as demonstrated by his reactions to Richie's freewheeling behaviour. He wants just to escape: 'I think I'm gonna get myself a nice place way the hell out in the country' (p. 27). Probably his worst limitation is that he fails to see the need for negotiation. After the Digger's haggling with him he says, almost in desperation, 'I'm not gonna fuckin' argue with you, . . . Friday I come in for the twelve' (p. 94).

The Greek's partners, Richie Torrey the Mafia's man and Miller Schabb the businessman, want to develop a legitimate business. Miller's abilities, which are mainly ones of persuasion, have opened up a whole new range of possibilities. The Greek is suspicious about developing, wanting to stay with what he can cope with: 'I'm different than you, Richie . . . there's certain things I can do and certain things that if I do them, I'm gonna get inna shit . . . ' (p. 42). Nowhere is this difference between the old- and new-style business more evident than in the scene where the Greek is telling Miller about his run-in with the Digger. When he hears that the Digger has said he will pay, Miller sees the problem as over – after all, the Greek originally said that the Digger would not pay. But the Greek is still obscurely troubled because the Digger argued and haggled: 'and then the son of a bitch practically tells me: go fuck myself. I think he did tell me, go fuck myself' (p. 100).

In Higgins's books the ability to use language as a weapon, to see it as a subtle variation of behaviour, is of the essence. When Richie is describing his troubles with the Greek to the Don he explains, 'Don . . . I have argued with him. I have tried to reason with him. I have even threatened him. He will not listen' (p. 123). It is only after that process has been gone through that the Don agrees to Richie killing the Greek. It is an ironic comment on the nature of violence that it is Richie who gets killed by the Greek, when he bungles the attempted assassination. Language and action are part of the same communication system, with language as the preferred, more sophisticated version. Richie has moved from killing to the more intricate modes of communication; even his sexual promiscuity is premised on communicative ability. When he is reduced to the simplicities of violence he loses out, to the expert.

But concentrating our attention on the exploration of communication in Higgins's books still leaves unanswered the question of what the skills of communication are for. Throughout Higgins's books runs the premise, stated either explicitly or implicitly, that communication supports the 'good order of the commonwealth'. Johnny Amato, like the Digger, has a gambling problem, it leads him to disrupt the established order of the criminal world, it becomes a problem that Cogan has to put right. Paul explains to the Digger that, even if there is no God, 'There's nothing wrong with the model of Christian life, even if there isn't any jackpot at the end. It's an orderly, dignified way to live, and that's not a bad thing' (p. 56).

What credit characters earn is derived from their support, however inadequately, of an 'orderly, dignified way to live'. Even Cogan draws a measure of sympathy, because he looks after a sick wife, stands by his boss Dillon, who is dying, and finally works out a Jacobean climax to preserve the order that Dillon has created. Even Jerry Fein supporting charities and seeking security for his family in old age wins a degree of concern, particularly since he is such an incompetent criminal.

It seems inevitable, especially with benefit of hindsight, that Higgins should have gone on to write books about politics. Politics is probably the supreme example of the interpretation of language and action, it is also about the interaction of written and spoken language. Politics as 'the art of the possible' is all about achieving a consensus between power and people; the results are then written down to regulate future conduct. Higgins explores the ways in which people arrive at objectives within different groups, and writes down the results, usually in the form of literature.

From the beginning he has his criminals involved, albeit marginally, in clandestine deals with political figures. In order for the Digger, an ex-convict, to be able to hold a licence for a bar a pardon has to be obtained. It is, in exchange for money. But more important is the awareness that the criminal society he writes about transacts its arrangements with the same range of communication weaponry that politics use. The title of Higgins's 1975 nonfiction book *The Friends of Richard Nixon* deliberately echoes that of his 1972 novel *The Friends of Eddie Coyle*.

Politics may be seen as the manipulation of discourse at all levels. Higgins's interest in the nature and working of discourse seems, looking back, to gravitate naturally through different social levels: low life, the law, politics. As far as I know, no book by Higgins has yet been devoted to religion, but, as Roman Catholicism figures as a counterpoint in many of the books, it seems an ideal candidate for exploration. Indeed, in *The Patriot Game* (1982) the Digger's long-suffering brother Paul, who is now a bishop, figures quite prominently.

Higgins's interest is in the way people handle the resources of language and action at their disposal. The difference in context means very little, since it is the same resources which are being scrutinised in each instance. Bernie Morgan in *A Choice of Enemies* is the Speaker of the House, but his power, like that of the Greek, is based in part on his ability to create physical fear. But, just as that ability of the Greek has become less relevant to the new business Mafia, so Bernie Morgan seems to many 'like a very heavy albatross around the necks of party stalwarts'.[11] This is not for a minute to suggest that Bernie Morgan is as limited as the Greek, but simply to point out that in different combinations the characters in the different books can be seen as exploring the resources of communication.

At the same time there is evaluation of those resources taking place, sometimes through the action, sometimes through overt commentary. When Frank Costello, the Speaker's adviser in *A Choice of Enemies*, is describing the realities of legislation to the ambitious Archambault, the latter interposes, 'Fixing, in other words.' Costello thinks for a while and then continues, 'Lobbying, . . . expediting, accommodating, adjusting: I've heard it called by lots of names. The names that sound evil are the ones used by the people at least temporarily unable to do it to their own benefit and to prevent other people from doing for themselves.'[12]

The political novels give scope for overt commentary such as this. In the crime novels it is less overt, often implicit rather than explicit, but commentary there still is. Later in the scene between the Digger and the driver that we have discussed in detail above we find the following exchange:

'. . . They don't keep any real dough there. It's just for intruders, is all.'

'Trespassers', the Digger said.

'Yeah', the driver said, 'trespassers. Speaking of which, I assume you're not a shitter or anything.'   (p. 7)

The Digger, obviously to the surprise of the driver, possibly even to flaunt his early success in their verbal duel, plays a variation on the word 'intruders': 'trespassers'. The driver has to agree to the validity of the variation but implicitly comments on it by returning the exchange to the fundamentals.

The driver's implied comment on the Digger's creativity brings us around to the second question on Higgins proposed earlier in this essay: so what? It is all very well attempting to demonstrate that his books can be read as explorations of the ways in which language and action can be used to communicate. In addition he investigates the ways in which the goal of communication is the preservation of some kind of stability within a given group. We are still left with the question, why novels? Surely the parallels pointed up between fiction and the real world echoed in *The Friends of Eddie Coyle* and *The Friends of Richard Nixon* are sufficient to call in question the novels. If the novels are simply a shadow of the 'real thing', it seems that they risk being no more than advertisements for a product we consume freely every time we communicate.

Hartman, in *Saving the Text*, describes Derrida's challenge to literature as the pronouncement that 'with the advent of writing the very notion of substance receives a wound as incurable as that which afflicts Amfortas in *Parsifal*'.[13] Not only does Higgins orphan his words by writing them down, but his manipulation of what appears to be 'real' language by authenticating devices removes words even further from their location in life. We find ourselves far removed from reality with a text open to endless polysemous readings of which this is one.[14] Hartman's attempt to 'save the text' is a demonstration 'that the reality of the effect is inseparable, in literature, from the reality of words that conduct voice–feeling'.[15] If written words have the power to wound by their lack of existence in hallowed ground, they also have the power to bless and make the ground of the book hallowed. 'Literature, I surmise, moves us beyond the fallacious hope that words can heal without also wounding. They are homeopathic, curing like by like . . .'[16]

This notion of texts as having the capacity to wound or heal seems to me particularly useful in commenting on Higgins's books. He uses the tradition of gangster books with their hard action, snappy dialogue and often simplistic morality to explore how people communicate. But he has also to be aware that to write novels about such matters is to run the risk of separating the writing from reality in an unbearable way.

To conclude this discussion I shall endeavour to suggest some ways in which I think Higgins heals the wounds his language opens up. Take for example this sentence from *The Friends of Eddie Coyle*: 'When the Ford was alone on the road, Dillon brought the revolver up and held it an inch behind Coyle's head, the muzzle pointing at the base of the skull behind the left ear.'[17] The scene is nothing unusual in a gangster thriller, what is possibly less usual is that it is the hero, or rather anti-hero, Coyle who is on the receiving end. The wound he receives, 'behind the left ear' does not at first sight seem like justice, poetic or otherwise. He is being executed for a betrayal he did not commit. But the wound by the ear is retributive in the sense that Eddie loses the sound of himself – the wound opens up an ear that was deafened to his own voice. After all, Eddie has some sympathy from us; he has obviously got the bad end of past deals, but up to the present his word has been his bond. When he says to the up-and-running gun-dealer Jackie Brown, 'Well, you're learning something too kid, and I advise you, you better learn it now, because when you say that, when you get me out there all alone on what you say, well, you better be there in back of me',[18] we see the necessity for such a credo but are troubled by its falsity, since Eddie is already dealing with the police to save his skin. The wound by the ear opens the aural pathway that was becoming a labyrinthine corridor from its possessor's spoken words to secret thoughts. The wound gives back Eddie his directness.

The actual betrayer of the bank robbers is Scalisi's girlfriend Wanda. Her betrayal of him is based on a dialogue of betrayals that he sets in motion. When Eddie calls with the guns, Scalisi talks about their intimate life together, something that she would never do to him. His defence is, 'She's mad because I tell the goddamned truth.'[19] But Scalisi's justification does not heal the wound he has created because he is partial in what 'truths' he chooses to tell. When Wanda talks to her friend Corporal Vardenais, she actually talks about the personas that Scalisi has invented to open bank accounts: 'I don't think any of them are real people, you know? I think they're all just him.'[20] Wanda does not really betray Scalisi at all; she simply tells Vardenais what Scalisi told her. The wound Scalisi has made is to turn their fucking-together into language: 'they don't say very much in front of me, except my friend likes to talk about fucking me in front of his friends, he does that, its okay to talk about that'.[21] Now Wanda is talking about Scalisi's secret life to her friend, the bitter dialogue is complete.

In *The Digger's Game* the robbery that gets the Digger out of his difficulties is 'blown' to the FBI by Harrington. Even in his betrayal of the Digger there is a kind of healing power. At the beginning of the book the Digger is telling Harrington about the Las Vegas trip. Harrington is sarcastic and scornful of what he sees as the naïveté of those who went on the trip. He is too smart in a cheap way; he has got 'a big mouth'. In spite of no desire on our part to see the Digger betrayed, it is confirmation of our estimate of Harrington's character of our response to his talk that it should be he who succumbs to greed. His talk is a crude instrument to gain small victories; our interpretation is justified by his talking to the FBI to get the reward money.

The final scene of *The Digger's Game* has the Digger and his wife going off to make love – ' "if it's all right with you", she said, "it's all right with me" '. It heals our sense of betrayal of the Digger, because it brings to a satisfying conclusion their very first scene together, where the Digger was unable to escape the limitations with which his wife was able to counter his every dialogue move. In their relationship with each other the wounds of language are turned to blessings.

Higgins's books, for all the criminality of their settings, are essentially healing. In both the language and the violence we recognise an exploration of abrasive human relationships. But our sense of closure is satisfied because the outcomes clearly derive from the logic of the various discourses the characters engage in. Art, unlike life, validates its expression by allowing us to recognise its fitness.

Notes

1. George V. Higgins, *A Choice of Enemies* (London: Secker and Warburg, 1984) p. 150.
2. Geoffrey H. Hartman, *Saving the Text* (Baltimore: Johns Hopkins University Press. 1981).
3. A selection of quotations taken from reviews from the *Daily Mirror*, the *Scotsman* and the *Observer* from 1972 to 1986 (printed on the dust-jackets).
4. George V. Higgins, *The Digger's Game* (London: Secker and War-burg, 1974). Quotations from the novel are from this edition. Page references are given in the text.
5. P. J. Rabinowitz, 'The Turn of the Glass Key: Popular Fiction as Reading Strategy', *Critical Inquiry*, 11, no. 3 (Mar 1985) 423.
6. G. H. Hartman, 'Literature High and Low', *The Fate of Reading and other Essays* (Chicago: Chicago University Press. 1975) pp. 214–15.
7. George V. Higgins, *The Friends of Jerry Coyle* (London: Secker and Warburg) p. 14.
8. George V. Higgins, *Cogan's Trade* (London, 1976) p. 191.
9. C. Lasch, *The Minimal Self: Psychic Survival in Troubled Times* (London: Pan, 1985) p. 72.
10. G. Bateson, 'Problems in Cetacean and Other Mammalian Com-munication', *Steps to an Ecology of Mind* (St Albans: Paladin, 1973) pp. 334–348 (quoting from pp. 336, 337).
11. Higgins, *A Choice of Enemies*, p. 5.
12. Ibid., p. 12.
13. Hartman, *Saving the Text*, p. 119.
14. There is an interesting discussion of the same issue in A. Easthope, 'The Problem of Polysemy and Identity in the Literary Text', *British Journal of Aesthetics*, 25, no. 4 (Autumn 1985) 326–39.
15. Hartman, *Saving the Text*, p. 1211.
16. Ibid., pp. 122–3.
17. Higgins, *The Friends of Jerry Coyle*, p. 155.
18. Ibid., p. 59.
19. Ibid., p. 99.
20. Ibid., p. 121.
21. Ibid., p. 124.

10

Exploding the Genre: The Crime Fiction of Jerome Charyn

MIKE WOOLF

In the good old days your average real-life murder was a woman coming into the apartment and finding her husband drunk again, and shaking him, and then saying the hell with it, and going out to the kitchen for an ice pick and sticking him sixteen times in the chest and the throat. That was real life, baby. You wanted bull shit, you went to mystery novels written by ladies who lived in Sussex. Thrillers. About as thrilling as Aunt Lucy's tattered nightcap.[1]

Ed McBain exhibits no great respect for the tradition of English detective fiction and he implies a radical distinction between American and English forms of the genre. While American practitioners present an almost exclusively urban world, the English model still flirts with a mythic landscape – a quasi-Edwardian rural England unbruised by contemporary experience. For the American writer, the landscape of crime is a fragmented, violent world where disorder is the norm. For the most part, in that environment the detective struggles to establish a temporary illusion of moral order within a permanently fractured universe. It is a holding operation in a world at the edge of catastrophe. The English counterpart tends to perceive crime as an aberration in an otherwise ordered world, and thus the task of the detective is to restore the moral and social cohesion which has been temporarily splintered. For a whole range of American writers, from Hammett and Chandler to McBain, Himes and Ross McDonald, death and disappearance are, in contrast, part of a shared notion of what constitutes the dangerous irrationality of contemporary experience. It is clear that the differences between the English and

131

American forms of the genre derive from radical differences in the way in which reality is perceived.

The texture and tone of the English form is still rooted in a world of secure social order enforced by a stable class structure. This is characterised by John Fowles in his excursion into the genre in his short story 'The Enigma'. The story concerns the mysterious disappearance of a wealthy Member of Parliament who divides his time between 'the usual things. His club. He was rather keen on the theatre. He dined out a lot with friends. He enjoyed an occasional game of bridge...'[2] and his home in the country, Tetbury Hall. Fowles typifies the prevailing mood in English detective fiction. It is nostalgic and elegaic, recalling a dreamed, lost world 'about as thrilling as Aunt Lucy's tattered nightcap' and not half as real.

In contrast, American reality, as Philip Roth argued in 1961, 'stupefies ... sickens ... infuriates, and finally it is even a kind of embarrassment to one's own meager imagination'.[3] That notion of a bizarre, disordered cosmos pervades American writing since the Second World War, and detective fiction, with its traditional motifs of violence and sudden death, offers a means of objectifying that perception of experience. Thus, criminal disorder can be seen to represent a recurrent version of everyday experience. The American detective genre, therefore, moves from the periphery of literary debate towards the centre precisely as its subject matter seems to offer more and more appropriate ways of perceiving a dangerously irrational reality.

Theoretically, then, the genre offers the potential for the development of an urban fiction which has as its real concern the texture of contemporary experience, that uses crime and criminality as metaphors for a reality in which social disorder, even evil, is a perceived norm. Within that structure, it is also appropriate that the detective should be a failed figure, precisely because his struggle is not so much with the criminal but with a prevailing notion of reality. He achieves, at best, a temporary illusion of control beneath which chaos prevails.

I am led, then, toward a notion of an exploding genre, a sense that the detective novel in America can become a vehicle for the exploration of the profane and the profound. In the work of Jerome Charyn, the radical potential within the genre is fully realised and the boundaries of the readers' expectations are deeply altered by the manner in which he both exploits and transcends the traditional preoccupations of the form.

Charyn is a prolific and inventive novelist who has, in eighteen books examined and dramatised what he sees as 'the terror, the loneliness, and the perversity of human experience.'[4] He has asserted that 'the contemporary writer has been left with little else than a sense of dislocation, a splintered reality, and the shards and bones of language.'[5] Further, he argues that 'the personae of our best writers drift through their fictive landscapes half-asleep, locked within the muted, disordered tones of the catatonic, in a dream-riddled violent world.'[6] The emphases on terror, loneliness, violence and dislocation clearly establish the parameters of Jerome Charyn's perception of reality. They also indicate why, in some of his work, the detective genre has offered an appropriate vehicle for the transmission of the fictional expression of that perception. His theoretical statements establish his position within the context of what Leslie Fiedler defined as the truly contemporary writer:

> The vision of the truly contemporary writer is that of a world not only absurd but also chaotic and fragmentary. He tries in his work to find techniques for representing a universe in which our perceptions overlap but do not coincide, in which we share chiefly a sense of loneliness: our alienation from whatever things finally are, as well as from other men's awareness of those things and of us. Rapid shifts in point of view; dislocations of syntax and logic; a vividness more like hallucination than photography; the use of parody and slapstick at moments of great seriousness – these experiments characterise much of the best work of recent decades. . . .[7]

Charyn has a very clear place, then, within the context of current and recent American literary experimentation with narrative and form. He also carries into that area another set of influences that serve to modify the theoretical notions of fragmentation and disjunction, that serve also to invigorate his writing within the detective genre. The experience of a Jewish childhood in New York is a rich source of regional particularity in his writing and serves, paradoxically, to root the rootlessness of his protagonists within a dense and concrete location. In the richest of senses, Charyn is a regional novelist: 'As far as the actual writing is concerned, both my strengths and backgrounds are very limited – a few blocks in the East Bronx were my complete universe. It was a provincial world, but I tried to shove as much sophistication as I could into that particular province.'[8] The combination of literary innovation and Jewish-American experience in his work has led to the development of a deeply personal mythology that is both reflective of contemporary fragmentation and responsive to the persistence of spiritual potential within the contemporary environment. He has, in short, sustained a radical conjunction of hell and heaven merging urban alienation with spiritual affirmation, straddling the line that links the contemporary American novel with traditional Jewish story-telling.

This makes Charyn a notoriously difficult novelist to categorise simply. He has written within a number of genres, transforming, for example, the shape of the campus novel in *The Tar Baby* (1973), and the Western in *Darlin' Bill: A Love Story of the Wild West* (1980). Between 1975 and 1978, he produced a detective tetralogy: *Blue Eyes* (1975), *Marilyn the Wild* (1976), *The Education of Patrick Silver* (1976) and *Secret Isaac* (1978). These were reordered to establish the chronological development of the plot and published in Britain as *The Isaac Quartet* (1984).

Much of the conventional furniture of New York-based detective fiction is apparent. There is, for example, a sustained awareness of ethnic multiplicity and a sense, as in Mario Puzo, that crime offers a pathway to material acquisition for ethnic groups largely excluded from the opportunities in mainstream WASP-dominated American capitalism. Don Corleone, for example, in Mario Puzo's *The Godfather*, is, in many respects, a kind of perverse Horatio Alger, a version of that most American of archetypes, the self-made man. He embodies an extreme manifestation of the free-enterprise system, and operates within a structure that is alternative to American society but is, in fact, a mirror image of it. This notion of ethnic criminality is particularly clearly stated in Jay Neugeboren's *Before My Life Began*:

> And what did Mr Rothenberg do wrong? Sell liquor to people when everyone was doing the same? Sure. Why was it legal when the state took your bet but illegal when someone else did it away from the track? 'I am only an American business man in a land of opportunity', he would say to me, and I believed he was right. . . . Except that the difference between him and the heads of the big banks and corporations was that he never took money out of poor people's mouths and he never ran sweatshops and

he never busted unions and he never had good people knocked off and he never lied to himself.[9]

Like Puzo's Italians, Neugeboren's Jews are a criminal mirror of American mainstream capitalism. That perception of ethnic criminality, with its implied critique of corporate America, is widespread in American writing, expressed, to a degree, in Chester Himes's portrayal of Harlem and even within Scott Fitzgerald's *The Great Gatsby*.

While encompassing this economic rationale for ethnic crime, Charyn goes a step further in his portrayal of the various groups. He represents New York as a tribal society populated by warring ethnic communities occupying clearly defined territories. These groups are deeply interwined in a system that blurs the boundaries between good and evil, detective and criminal. The nature of the perceived world is narrowed in a geographical and social sense. Only cops and criminals populate the city. However, in another sense, the perception of the world is expanded beyond the materialist norm associated with the portrayal of ethnic crime.

In *Blue Eyes*, for example, Detective Isaac pursues a criminal gang of crypto-Jews, the Marranos. The head of the clan, Papa Guzmann, mourns the deaths of Detective Coen, Blue Eyes, and the criminal Chinaman who was the cause of his death. Papa expresses a notion of reality that combines urban violence with spiritual persistence. For the Guzmann clan, and within the texture of Charyn's fictional universe, the existence of 'destructive angels' is no more problematic than the existence of a pursuing 'shotgun brigade'. The city streets contain both mayhem and magic. The motifs of the detective novel are employed to represent a view of reality as spiritually charged as that of Isaac Bashevis Singer's:

Papa burned candles for the Chinaman and Coen on the shelf above his malted machines. He prayed to Moses with a dishrag on his skull, spat three times according to Marrano law, so Coen and the Chinaman might be able to rest in purgatory. . . . The dead needed whole families to intercede for them, brothers, sisters, fathers, nephews, mothers, sons, to wear dishrags and shawls, to offer pennies to the Christian Saints, to appease Moses with a candle, to recite Hebrew prayers transcribed into sixteenth century Portugese. Coen and the Chinaman were familyless man without the Marrano knack to survive. Papa discarded any notions of immortality for himself. He had lived like a dog, biting the noses of his enemies, smelling human shit on two continents, sleeping in a crouch to safeguard his vulnerable parts, and he expected to drop like a dog, with blood in his rectum, and somebody's teeth in his neck. But Papa didn't intend to die from an overdose of Isaac, or offer his sons to the First Deputy's shotgun brigade. He believed Isaac was more than a simple son-of-a-bitch. What cop would want to erase six Guzmanns, almost an entire species of men? Isaac had to be one of those destructive angels sent by the Lord Adonai to torment pigeaters, the Marranos who had slipped between Christians and Jews for so many years they could no longer exist without Moses *and* Jesus (or John the Baptist) in their beds, and had defied the laws of Adonai with their foreskins and their rosaries.

(p. 277[10])

Papa Guzmann's perceptions are not aberrations or psychological quirks. They represent a radical perception of urban reality in which the conjunction of the profane and the profound is characteristic of the fictional environment. Isaac is, in an actual sense, more than a 'simple son-of-a-bitch' detective. His identity is shifting and ambiguous. When Isaac wears disguise, it reflects more than conventional police procedure. It symbolises the multiplicity of selves contained within the single figure. It is a reflection of the potential for transformation, the degree to which Isaac is, for Papa Guzmann, 'a destructive angel', the messenger of an avenging God, and a shape out of a religious nightmare: 'Isaac was Papa's devil' (p. 310). Charyn thus employs and transforms the motifs of detective fiction. He represents violence, crime, death, pursuit and punishment while simultaneously extending the significance of the ostensible subject matter of the fiction. The central figure of Isaac is an investigating detective and a sequence of alternative identities – at times, the grieving father searching for his lost daughter and his dead, surrogate son, and, at times, a wounded prophet, a protector–defender of the dispossessed, and a dark angel bringing death. Within the single figure, a sense of the physical and metaphysical nature of reality is sustained.

The multiple identities of Isaac are crucial in the novel. He is a kind of failed Sherlock Holmes of the soul. In *Marilyn the Wild*, Isaac is at the centre of a network of fathers. He searches for his own, and seeks and fails to protect his wayward daughter and

Coen, his surrogate son. He moves between the position of a child 'giggling like an idiot boy who'd escaped from his father's house' (p. 19) and 'Isaac, the Pure', humanised by suffering and compassion, the Old Testament patriarch and protector of the dispossessed: 'Marilyn smiled from her grandmother's doorway. Isaac was plagued by a swarm of relatives, like any Jewish patriarch. He supplied the family glue. The Sidels would have crumbled long ago without the ministrations of Isaac. He soothed, he slapped, he mended broken wires, Marilyn's incredible daddy' (p. 94).

Isaac is both father and son, an embodiment of a network of child–parent relationships that criss-cross throughout the novels in a deeply complex manner, creating a field of emotional interaction and turmoil. Coen, for example, is an orphan in search of his dead parents, and a surrogate son for Isaac. He becomes involved with Isaac's daughter, Marilyn, who is attempting to escape from Isaac. The whole creates a sense of tension between searching fathers and lost and escaping children. Marilyn, the lost child, comforts Coen, the grieving orphan: 'She licked him clean, until he lost the nervous shivers of a cop. She wasn't a dreamy girl. She understood Coen's obligations, his loyalty to her father, his somber ways. She hadn't slept with too many orphans before Coen. She wouldn't have believed a man could hold his dead father and mother in the furrows of his chin' (p. 120). The complex interweaving of parent–child relationships permeates the novels and Isaac's role is to dramatise those relationships, to pursue a solution to the insoluble, to seek to find answers to the turmoil of fragmented parent–child relationships. Isaac thus begins to represent a recurrent concern in Jewish-American writing, the alienation of generation from generation.

In *Secret Isaac*, his attempts to solve a crime are futile precisely because the 'crime' is a metaphor of the fragmentation and breakdown characteristic of this view of human relationships. Isaac's struggle becomes a profound and doomed search for cohesion and meaning in an incoherent universe that defies understanding. He becomes 'a cop who makes his own religion' (p. 506), an inventor of metaphors to comprehend the incomprehensible, a figure whose suffering marks him as a kind of mad prophet separated, like Melville's Ahab, from the bulk of mankind because of his terrible knowledge of evil and goodness: 'Isaac's eyeballs were inflamed. He looked like some Ahab hunting whales in an old, dry building. A crease appeared in the middle of his forehead. His seven days of mourning had isolated him from all humankind. The hairs stood on his scalp like an idiot's knot' (p. 508). Isaac's failure is assured precisely because he seeks to find answers to the unanswerable. His investigations in Paris and Dublin are, in fact, investigations into the tortured and impotent soul.

Isaac is thus transformed into a version of a holy fool – a figure recurrent in Jewish mythology. He both perceives the futile madness of the surrounding world, and defies it, operating within a sense of universal psychosis and, simultaneously, outside it, groping blindly toward some version of God's grace:

> 'It's ungovernable', Isaac said. '. . . this terrain. Psychosis is everywhere . . . in your armpit . . . under your shoe. You can smell it in the sweat in this room . . . we're all baby killers, repressed or not . . . how do you measure a man's rage? Either we behave like robots, or we kill. Why do you expect your Police Force to be any less crazy than you?'
>
> There was laughter in the room, some hissing.   (p. 400)

Isaac perceives that the police are part of a deranged cosmos, and yet, as the philosopher–cop, he continues to act as if there existed the possibility of redemption and salvation. As a would-be protector of the dispossessed, he walks in the land of the dead, a doomed futile figure carrying within a tapeworm which is his own sense of guilt, impotence and suffering: 'He crept into the coverlets, a frightened dog-boy with hair on his arms and a wild fur over the rest of his body.... He had a foulness in his heart. The dead seemed to follow Isaac. They wouldn't lie still. He'd buried Coen, he'd buried Annie Powell. He brought rabbis in for them. What more could he do?' (p. 531). He emerges as a new form of detective hero. His 'heroism' is based precisely on failure not success, on suffering not the alleviation of the condition. He is a 'hero' because he both recognises his own impotence within the prevailing psychosis, and struggles against it in massively futile persistence. Charyn's Isaac Sidel is an embodiment of the epigram cited by Nathanael West in *The Dream Life of Balso Snell*: 'The semites are like to a man sitting in a cloaca to the eyes, and whose brows touch heaven.'[11]

Through the figure of Isaac, Charyn has expanded the subject matter of the detective novel while maintaining its essential energy. He creates a landscape that reflects our perception of contemporary urban disorder and is simultaneously full of ethnic and spiritual complexity. This can further be seen through the manner in which Charyn exploits the ambiguity of police idiom. The words 'angel' and 'rabbi' are used to signify various relation-ships within the police, but Charyn also sustains their literal sense, suggesting a dualism in the nature of reality. Thus, Cowboy's plight in *Marilyn the Wild* is both due to his lack of a patron and a result of the absence of an otherworldly protector: 'The world wasn't right. Cowboy had been passed over by whichever angel distributed charity to fathers in the boroughs of New York' (p. 113). Similarly, Coen's rise to prominence comes out of Isaac's intervention, as Coen's 'rabbi' in both potential senses of the word:

> After graduation the First Dep picked him up. Coen had a rabbi now. Isaac assigned him to the First Dep's special detective squad. Half a year later Coen had a gold badge. He rose with Isaac the Chief, making first grade at the age of twenty-nine. . . . He was the department's wonderboy until his rabbi fell from grace. (pp. 145–6)

Thus, failure and success are, through the manipulation of the language, seen in dualistic terms, the result of machinations within the police force and, implicitly, as symptoms of an alternative reality where quasi-divine intervention is a social fact.

Charyn grafts onto the forms of the detective novel a set of deeply personal strategies which permit the mystical transform-ations that are characteristic of his view of reality. As an essential part of his method, he transforms the familiar through, particu-larly, the use of incongruous conjunctions. The world is made strange, as in this description of Selma Paderowski's courtship of the idiot boy, Jerónimo Guzmann: 'Selma Paderowski, thirteen, and a drinker of chocolate sodas, squinted at Jerónimo's woolly grey hair and decided to be in love. Proving her affection she tossed rocks at him, tore pieces of his shirt, dared him to peek at her crack' (p. 183). The narrative throughout presents the oddness of the experiences described without any sense of surprise. Thus, there is no difficulty in defining character through the habit of drinking chocolate sodas, nor is there any contradiction in the conjunction of affection and tossing rocks. No narrative distinction is made between the bizarre and the mundane and the reader is, consequently, seduced into a state of consciousness where no such distinction exists. The strategy, of course, also permits the integration of the mundane with the mystical within a single version of everyday reality.

The contrast in narrative method between Charyn and the more conventional practitioners is clearly marked in a comparison between Mario Puzo's description of Carlo Rizzi's murder in *The Godfather* and the description of Isidoro's murder in *The Education of Patrick Silver*. In both cases, the victims are being punished for the betrayal of the family.

The car pulled away, moving swiftly towards the gate. Carlo started to turn his head to see if he knew the man sitting behind him. At that moment, Clemenza, as cunningly and daintily as a little girl slipping a ribbon over the head of a kitten, threw his garotte around Carlo Rizzi's neck. The smooth rope cut into the skin with Clemenza's powerful yanking throttle, Carlo Rizzi's body went leaping into the air like a fish on a line, but Clemenza held him fast, tightening the garotte until the body went slack. Suddenly there was a foul odour in the air of the car. Carlo's body, sphincter released by approaching death, had voided itself. [12]

Puzo's description depends, for the most part, on the use of incongruous simile ('as a little girl' and 'like a fish on a line') and on the detailed description with recurrent use of verbs of movement.

Whereas Puzo emphasises the bizarre and violent elements of the event, Charyn stresses the normality of the bizarre:

'Isidoro, you shouldn't have taken Isaac the Shit for a sweetheart. Why didn't you sing to a different cop? . . . '

Jorge clapped his elbow under the bagman's mouth. Isidoro didn't writhe against Jorge's chest. His eyeballs didn't have a bloody expression. The veins didn't rise on Isidoro's cheeks in slow, horrible clusters of blue. The bones cracked once behind his ears, and the bagman was dead. (p. 295)

For the most part Charyn's description is based upon what did not happen, and thus the event is neutralised and the reader is not permitted to visualise Isidoro's death. Whereas Puzo emphasises the dramatic nature of the event, Charyn presents the violence in a non-dramatic manner because it is seen to be a symptom and expression of mundane, everyday reality.

Within that climate, Charyn evolves a sense of the potential for transformations that evoke a reverberation of the mystic and the spiritual. Much of this derives, as I have argued, from the multiple and shifting nature of Isaac's identities. He is variously Isaac 'the Pure', 'the Shit', 'the Rabbi', 'the Brave', and so on. These 'disguises' are manifestations of Charyn's view of the complexity of human nature, its ambiguity, which can contain both the deeply flawed and the magical. This process of transformation, expressed through shifting nature of identity, is used throughout the novels. In *The Education of Patrick Silver*, for example, transformations are used for two specific purposes: first, to express a spiritual dimension within disordered urban reality, and then to generate a sense of mythic potential within everyday experience. An ex-detective, Patrick Silver, is protector of Jerónimo Guzmann and janitor of a synagogue – a ragged giant who becomes 'Patrick of the Synagogues: apostle of the rough' (p. 356). Throughout, characters acquire titles in a manner that implies transformation of status, a mythical complexity: Marilyn is 'the Wild', Coen 'Blue Eyes', Dermott Bride becomes 'the King'. The detective novel is employed to present a process of transformation where character moves toward myth, where particulars of personality give way to broad, quasi-heroic projections. The novels present an accumulating sense of urban epic.

By the final novel in the tetralogy, Charyn moves most clearly toward a combination of urban detective fiction and myth-making. Some of the action of *Secret Isaac* is set in Dublin, and the novel tells of Isaac's anguished guilt as he searches for the dead Coen, and of his futile attempt to protect the doomed prostitute Annie Powell. Charyn places the novel against Joyce's *Ulysses*, giving Isaac the alias of Moses Herzog. Dublin becomes a synthesis of a crime-ridden urban environment and a literary landscape where Isaac, mirroring the condition of Leopold Bloom, becomes a father in search of his lost children. The city is 'a fogtown that sprang out of James Joyce' (p. 427). Dublin exists, then, both as a real city and as a literary antecedent, and Charyn establishes a transaction between Joyce's Dublin and the New York underworld – both imagined in the shape of quasi-surrealistic nightmares. The novel records 'the history of Isaac after his fall from grace.'[13] In what is almost a city of the dead, Sidel, now a Bloom-type figure, wanders the city in search of the dead Coen and finally 'he becomes Coen and barks his own song of innocence and experience'.[14] In short, Isaac is transformed and humanised through suffering in a context that is literary, quasi-mythical and, simultaneously, a concrete representation of contemporary urban conditions.

The four novels establish a profound sense of the complexity of experience that encompasses terror and loneliness, and the possibilities of redemption and regeneration. Together they form a complex epic that moves among literary sources, criminal reality and self-generated mythology. The whole offers a fertile vision of a world where those elements are deeply integrated.

Charyn has taken the detective-novel genre and employed many of its traditional strategies, the fast narrative pace and the emphasis on plot in particular. In that respect, his work corresponds to the kind of assumptions about the genre that are implicit in Ed McBain's view. However, Charyn is not essentially concerned with the mechanics of crime and criminality. Those offer a set of metaphors through which he can approach the profoundest of paradoxes, the persistence of a notion of redemption in an ostensibly doomed and damned world. Within the violent disorder of contemporary experience, Charyn perceives the heroic nature of flawed humanity as it crawls towards some bizarre version of spiritual salvation. With these novels, Charyn explodes the boundaries of the genre.

Notes

1. Ed McBain, *Long Time No See* (London: Pan, 1979) p. 203.
2. John Fowles, 'The Enigma', in *The Ebony Tower* (London: Cape, 1974) p. 203.
3. Philip Roth, 'Writing American Fiction', in *Reading Myself and Others* (London: Cape, 1975) p. 120.
4. Jerome Charyn (ed.), Introduction to *The Single Voice* (New York: Collier-Macmillan, 1969) p. xi.
5. Jerome Charyn (ed.), Introduction to *The Troubled Vision* (New York: Collier-Macmillan, 1970) p. ix.
6. Ibid., p. x.
7. Leslie Fiedler, *No! In Thunder* (London: Eyre and Spottiswoode, 1963) p. 17.
8. Letter to the author, 1982.
9. Jay Neugeboren, *Before My Life Began* (New York: Simon and Schuster, 1985) p. 177.

10. Page references in the text relate to Jerome Charyn, *The Isaac Quartet* (London: Zomba Books, 1984). All quotations from the tetralogy are from this edition.

11. Nathanael West, *The Dream Life of Balso Snell*, in *The Complete Works of Nathanael West* (London: Secker and Warburg, 1968) p. 8.

12. Mario Puzo, *The Godfather* (London: Pan 1969) p. 439.

13. Jerome Charyn, 'Blue Eyes and the Barber King: An Introduction', in *The Isaac Quartet*, p. viii.

14. Ibid.

Select Bibliography

Barzun, Jacques, and Taylor, W. H., *Catalogue of Crime* (New York: Harper and Row, 1971).

Cawelti, John G., *Adventure, Mystery and Romance* (Chicago: University of Chicago Press, 1976).

Chandler, Frank A., *The Literature of Roguery*, 2 vols (Boston, Mass.: Houghton Mifflin, 1907).

Frohock, W. M., *The Novel of Violence in America* (Dallas: Southern Methodist University Press, 1957).

Gregory, Sinda, *Private Investigations: The Novels of Dashiell Hammett* (Carbondale: Southern Illinois University Press, 1985).

Harper, Ralph, *The World of the Thriller* (Cleveland, Ohio: Case Western Reserve University Press, 1969).

Haycraft, Howard, *Murder for Pleasure: The Life and Times of the Detective Story* (New York: Appleton-Century, 1941).

Keating, H. R. F. (ed.), *Crime Writers* (London: BBC, 1978).

Keating, H. R. F. (ed), *Whodunit* (London: Windmarch, 1982).

Knight, Stephen, *Form and Ideology in Crime Fiction* (London: Macmillan, 1980).

Madden, David (ed.), *Tough Guy Writers of the Thirties* (Carbondale: Southern Illinois University Press, 1968).

Mandel, Ernest, *Delightful Murder: A Social History of the Crime Story* (London: Pluto, 1984).

Moretti, Franco, *Signs Taken for Wonders* (London: Verso, 1983).

Murch, A. E., *The Development of the Detective Novel* (London: Peter Owen, 1968).

Palmer, Jerry, *Thrillers: Genesis and Structure of a Popular Genre* (London: Edward Arnold, 1978).

Penzler, Otto and Steinbrumer Chris, *Encyclopedia of Mystery and Detection* (London: Routledge and Kegan Paul, 1976).

Penzler, Otto with Steinbrumer, Chris, and Lachman, Marvin, *Detectionary: Biographical Dictionary of Leading Characters in Mystery Fiction* (Woodstock: Overlook Press, 1977).

Porter, Dennis, *The Pursuit of Crime: Art and Ideology in Detective Fiction* (New Haven, Conn.: Yale University Press, 1981).

Reuhlmann, William, *Saint with a Gun: The Unlawful American Private Eye* (New York: New York University Press, 1974).

Symons, Julian, *Bloody Murder* (New York: Viking, 1985).

Watson, Colin, *Snobbery with Violence* (London: Eyre and Spottiswoode, 1971).

Winks, Robin, W. (ed.) *Detective Fiction: A Collection of Essays* (Englewood Cliffs, N. J.: Prentice-Hall, 1980).

Winn, Dilys, *Murder Ink* (Newton Abbot: Westbridge Books, 1978).

Worpole, Ken, *Dockers and Detectives* (London: Verso, 1983).

Index